ZENA SKINNER'S
DOWN TO EARTH
COOKBOOK

ZENA SKINNER'S

DOWN TO EARTH
~•~ COOKBOOK ~•~

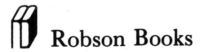 Robson Books

FIRST PUBLISHED IN GREAT BRITAIN IN 1982 BY ROBSON
BOOKS LTD., BOLSOVER HOUSE, 5-6 CLIPSTONE STREET,
LONDON W1P 7EB. COPYRIGHT © 1982 ZENA SKINNER.

*For the chapters on vegetarian and diabetic recipes we are grateful for the
assistance given by the Vegetarian Society and the British Diabetic Association.*

British Library Cataloguing in Publication Data
Skinner, Zena
  Zena Skinner's down to earth cookbook.
  1. Cookery
  I. Title
  641.5   TX 652

ISBN 0 86051 159 6

Produced by David Booth (Publishing) Limited
Illustrations by Stonecastle Graphics
Photographs by David Davies, courtesy of the Potato Marketing Board

Printed in Hungary.

CONTENTS

MEAT (Miscellaneous)

POULTRY AND GAME

SALADS

PUDDINGS (Hot)

PUDDINGS (Cold)

LUNCH AND SUPPER

CAKES (Large)

CAKES (Small)

BISCUITS

PASTRIES

INTRODUCTION

I have written this book as a tribute to my Mother who was an excellent cook and patiently guided me into the world of cooking.

I know that she, like me, would hope that this book will interest people who are not only learning to cook but those who are already enjoying cooking too.

· As its name implies, the text and recipes are very much 'Down to Earth' or everyday recipes of the kind I think most families would enjoy.

Wherever possible I have used fresh ingredients which are full of goodness and more often than not the cheapest.

Over the years I have had many requests for Vegetarian and Diabetic recipes so I am happy to include a number of them at the end of this book.

There is a short introduction to each section of recipes which will, I hope, whet your appetites. To make your selection as easy as possible each recipe is in alphabetical order within its section.

My grateful thanks to my family who have patiently tested all these recipes with me without complaint, to my friends who typed all the recipes and spent long hours proof reading, and finally to everyone connected with the production of this book.

Have fun with your cooking!

ZENA SKINNER

Metric Weights and Measures

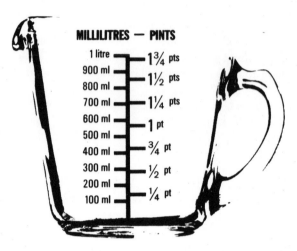

GOLDEN RULE

Never mix metric and the old imperial measures in one recipe. Stick to one system or the other.

BASIC PRINCIPLES

I am devoting the first chapter of this book to the definition of sixteen Basic Principles of Cookery, all of which occur in some of the recipes to be found in the ensuing pages.

I hope they will be of use to you as a quick reference, and no doubt they will be of particular interest to those of you who are just starting to cook.

BAKING BLIND

This means to line a flan ring with pastry and bake it without a filling. There are various ways to do this and it is usual to prick the base of the pastry with a fork.

Once this has been done place a piece of greaseproof paper in the base of the flan and cover it with dried peas, rice or crusts of bread.

Alternatively, an easier way these days to bake blind is to put two or three thicknesses of foil in the base of the flan case before baking.

Whichever method is used the case is then baked and filled later, either with a cold filling or one that has to be set in the oven.

BATTERS

A mixture of flour, eggs, milk, etc. It can be a sweet or savoury batter and varies in consistency according to its use. There are two main types.

Thin Batter
This is used for such dishes as Yorkshire pudding and pancakes to name just two. It should be of a pouring consistency and therefore can be likened to thin cream.

When poured from a jug or dropped from a spoon, it should spread quickly.

Thick Batter

Used in the making of such recipes as drop scones or Scotch pancakes. It should be of a pouring consistency of thick cream. In this case it spreads slowly when dropped from a spoon.

YORKSHIRE PUDDING

Ingredients

4 oz plain flour
pinch salt
$\frac{1}{2}$ pint milk and water
1 egg
1 oz dripping or lard

METHOD

Sieve flour and salt into a basin and make a well in the centre. Add the egg and about one-third of the liquid and mix to a smooth batter with a wooden spoon.

Gradually add the remaining liquid, beating well all the time.

Leave batter to stand for about 15 minutes to soften.

Heat the dripping or lard in the roasting pan and when smoking hot, pour in the batter.

Bake near the top of the oven at 425°F (220°C) or mark 7 for 25–35 minutes, or until well risen and crisp golden brown.

PANCAKES

METHOD

Use the same batter as for the Yorkshire Pudding.

Heat very little lard in a small frying pan, until smoking hot.

Pour in sufficient batter to just cover the base of the pan.

Cook until golden brown on the underside then turn over or toss on to the other side and cook in the same way.

Sprinkle with lemon juice and caster sugar, roll up and serve with wedges of lemon and extra sugar. (6–8 pancakes)

COATING BATTER

Ingredients

4 oz plain flour
pinch salt
pinch pepper
1 egg
¼ pint milk and water

METHOD

Make in the same way as the Yorkshire Pudding batter.

Dip the washed and dried fillets of fish in seasoned flour, then coat in batter before frying.

FRITTER BATTER

Ingredients

2 oz plain flour
pinch salt
½ gill tepid water
1 dessertspoonful olive oil
1 egg white

METHOD

Sieve flour and salt into a basin and mix to a smooth batter with the water and oil.

Cover and leave to stand in a cool place for about 30 minutes.

Whisk egg white stiffly and fold into batter.

Use for coating apple rings, halved bananas and well drained and dried pineapple rings.

Fry in sufficient fat to allow the food to float and test the temperature of the fat by dropping a cube of bread into the fat. If the bread comes to the surface slowly and then starts to brown the fat is at the right temperature.

BEATING AND CREAMING

Beating

A method of mixing air into food by vigorous motion, i.e. turning the mixture over and over with a wide circular movement.

A wooden spoon or spatula is best for beating thick mixtures such as fat and sugar; and an egg whisk is best for thin mixtures such as eggs and cream.

Creaming

This is the beating of softened fat or fat and sugar until it is light and fluffy, that is to say the consistency of whipped cream.

BLANCHING

The literal meaning of blanching is to whiten. In this context it means the removal of skins from almonds, tomatoes or peaches.

To skin almonds – put them in a basin, pour over boiling water for a few minutes, then into cold water before skinning.

Tomatoes and peaches are held on a fork, dipped into boiling water for a few minutes, then plunged into cold water. This causes the skin to shrink and thus makes it easy to remove.

BRAISING AND MARINADING

Braising

This is a combination of stewing and roasting on a bed of vegetables two inches in depth, using a deep saucepan with a well-fitting lid, or a casserole and sufficient liquid barely to cover the vegetables.

It's an ideal method for cooking small joints, the cheaper cuts of meat, game and poultry, as it is economical and produces its own gravy.

The meat is served garnished with the vegetables and the gravy is served separately.

Marinade

A mixture of oil and vinegar in equal quantities with herbs, spices and seasoning added. Alternatively use red or white wine with seasoning.

Marinade meat or fish, from one to twenty-four hours, this will improve the flavour, give more moisture when cooked and break down the tissue.

Meat and fish placed in a marinade should be kept cool and covered. The marinade should not cover the food and therefore it wants turning or basting frequently.

TO BRUSH AND GLAZE

In the baking of pies, buns and pastry, to 'brush with egg or milk' means to coat all over the surface with beaten egg or milk.

This is done before the dishes are put into the oven and when baked they have a shiny golden brown appearance, which makes the dish look more appetizing.

To Glaze

In baking this term generally applies to brushing the tops of pies, buns and pastry to improve the look and surface of the finished dish.

They are usually brushed with egg and water or sugar and water.

COATING

The literal meaning is to cover with a thin layer.

A number of recipes in this book say 'Coat with egg and breadcrumbs'.

The method is to beat the egg and therefore blend the white with the yolk. Dip the food into the beaten egg, lift it up and drain off any excess. Then toss in sufficient breadcrumbs to just coat the food all over.

Remove any surplus breadcrumbs before cooking, otherwise they will drop off during cooking.

TO DICE

The two essentials for this process are a chopping board and a really sharp knife.

It means cutting into small cubes. With regard to vegetables such as carrots and onions, cut long slices along the vegetable, then at right angles, but not right to the end, as the slices will hold together much better this way.

Finally, holding the vegetable firmly, cut across into cubes.

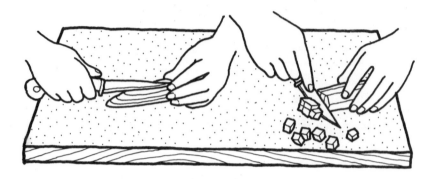

FILLETING (Fish)

This is the removal of the main bone from a fish.

Put the fish on to a chopping board and with a really sharp knife slit the fish down the backbone.

Separate the flesh from the backbone on each side by keeping the knife close to the bone.

By the way, use the fish bones and trimmings to make a fish stock. This when strained can be used in the making of soups and sauces.

FOLDING

This is a method of mixing flour or sugar into a beaten mixture and at the same time preserving the air already beaten in.

The full title, 'Cut and Fold' is, as its name implies, what has to be done. The edge of the spoon is used to cut through the mixture and it is then very slowly and gently turned over with the bowl of the spoon.

'Until evenly blended' means until all the flour or sugar has been folded into the mixture, and no traces of either can be seen. Take time folding to ensure an even texture.

GRATING

This means to shave into small shreds with the aid of a grater. Usually divided into 3 sections, i.e. Coarse – Medium – Fine.

Uses: Coarse – chiefly for vegetables, suet and in some cases cheese and apple.
Medium – breadcrumbs, orange- and lemon-rind, cheese and onion.
Fine – Nutmeg.

An easy way to clean the grater after use and therefore save waste, is to brush it with a pastry brush.

KNEADING AND DOUGHS

This is a process whereby a dough is worked lightly with the knuckles of the hands. The outside of the dough is brought into the centre and is kneaded with the knuckles.

'Mix to a Stiff Dough' is a term often used in the making of pastry and some biscuit mixtures. It means – add only sufficient liquid to bind all the ingredients together.

'Mix to a Soft Dough' is the term often used in the making of scones and yeast mixtures. In this case add sufficient liquid to make a soft pliable dough, which can be kneaded or rolled out, without being too soft to handle, i.e. if held by the fingers it should slowly drop.

PASTRY – CHOUX

A mixture of flour, salt, margarine, water and eggs. The proportions for 12–14 Cream Puffs are:—

$2\frac{1}{2}$ **oz plain flour**
pinch salt
2 oz margarine
$\frac{1}{4}$ **pint water**
2 eggs

Before you start pre-heat the oven to 425°F (220°C) or mark 7.

The method is simple – sieve the flour and salt.

Bring the margarine and water to the boil over a medium heat. Remove the pan from the heat, add the flour and beat until smooth.

Return the pan to a low heat and beat with a wooden spoon for 1–2 minutes, until the mixture leaves the side of the pan. Cool slightly.

Lightly whisk the eggs together and gradually beat into the cooled mixture until perfectly blended.

The mixture is now ready to use. Using a $\frac{1}{2}$-in. plain tube in a piping bag, pipe small round shapes on to greased baking tins. Bake at above temperature for 15 minutes then reduce to 375°F (190°C) or mark 5 for a further 20–25 minutes. When cold split and fill with whipped cream.

PASTRY – ROUGH PUFF AND FLAKY

A mixture of flour, fat and water, i.e. plain flour, lard and margarine, or butter in the proportions of three-quarters fat to flour, i.e. 12 oz of plain flour, $4\frac{1}{2}$ oz of lard for shortening and $4\frac{1}{2}$ oz of margarine or butter for browning. The methods for making the two pastries are different so I will deal with them separately.

Rough Puff
Cut the fat into the flour until it is in small pieces about the size of a pea, and mix to a stiff dough with cold freshly drawn water.

Roll out into a rectangle about $\frac{1}{4}$-in. thick keeping a good shape. Fold the top one-third down and the bottom, one-third up, then seal the open edges with a rolling pin. Give one turn to the right and repeat the rolling, folding and turning three more times. The pastry is then ready for use as required.

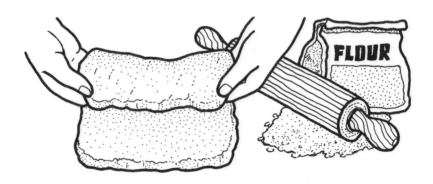

Flaky

Sieve the flour and salt into a basin. Blend the lard and butter or margarine together with a knife or fork, then divide into four equal portions.

Rub a quarter of the fat into the flour and mix to a stiff dough with cold water. Set aside in a cool place for half an hour.

Roll this mixture out into a rectangle about $\frac{1}{4}$-in. thick. Using a further quarter of the fat, place it in small lumps on two-thirds of the pastry. Fold into three making sure that the one-third without any fat is in the centre. Seal open edges with a rolling pin and give one turn to the right.

Roll out and repeat this process twice more. Finally roll and fold without adding any fat and turn; by now the pastry has been turned right round to the starting position.

Now the pastry is ready for use as required.

PASTRY – SHORTCRUST

A mixture of flour, salt, fat and water, i.e. plain flour, lard and margarine or butter in the proportions of half fat to flour, i.e.: 8 oz plain flour, 2 oz of lard for shortening and 2 oz of margarine or butter for browning and a pinch of salt.

The method for making this is very simple.

Sieve the flour and salt into a basin. Cut the fat into the flour until it is in small pieces about the size of a pea, then rub it into the flour with the tips of the fingers until it resembles fine breadcrumbs.

Add freshly drawn cold water and mix it with a round bladed knife, using a cutting and pressing movement, until it leaves the sides of the basin clean. Use as required.

PASTRY – SUET CRUST

A mixture of flour, salt, suet and water in the proportions of half suet to flour, i.e. 8 oz plain flour, a pinch of salt, 4 oz shredded suet or finely chopped suet and cold water to mix.

To make simply sieve the flour and salt together, add the suet and mix well. Gradually add the water to make a fairly soft dough. Knead lightly on a floured board, then roll out and use as required.

ROUX AND BLENDING

Roux

A mixture of flour and fat cooked together for 1 to 2 minutes as a basis of a sauce. The proportions of fat and flour vary according to the type of sauce required, i.e. pouring, coating or binding.

The flour and fat are cooked together without browning for a white sauce. To make a brown sauce they are cooked together until brown to give the sauce colour.

Blending

The combining of two or more ingredients. When making a sauce the liquid is gradually blended into the roux, with the pan off the heat. This ensures a smooth sauce and an even texture.

RUBBING IN

'Rub the fat into the flour until it resembles fine breadcrumbs' is a term frequently used in cookery preparation. Probably the most common use of this phrase is in the making of Short Crust Pastry.

It means rubbing the fat into flour using the tips of the fingers. By lifting the mixture up as you do this, it will incorporate air into the mixture. This process is continued until it resembles fine breadcrumbs, and is therefore thoroughly blended.

SAUCES
BASIC WHITE

POURING
$\frac{3}{4}$ oz plain flour
$\frac{3}{4}$ oz butter or margarine
$\frac{1}{2}$ pint liquid
salt and pepper

COATING
1 oz plain flour
1 oz butter or margarine
$\frac{1}{2}$ pint liquid
salt and pepper

BINDING
2 oz plain flour
2 oz butter or margarine
$\frac{1}{2}$ pint liquid
salt and pepper

The liquid can be all milk, milk and water or milk and the liquid the food has been cooked in, i.e. fish or vegetable stock.

Cook the fat and flour together for approximately 1 minute until all the fat has been absorbed by the flour.

Remove the pan from the heat and gradually add the liquid, beating well to give the sauce a good gloss.

Return the pan to the heat and slowly bring to the boil, stirring all the time. Season carefully and use as required.

Further flavourings may be added such as chopped hard-boiled egg, grated cheese, mustard, parsley, anchovy essence, etc.

To make a brown sauce simply cook the fat and flour together until brown in colour and proceed as for the white sauce.

Use sauces to provide moisture in dishes, improve the flavour, provide colour and aid the digestion.

STEAMING

This means cooking food in or over the steam from boiling water. There are three methods:

(a) By direct contact with the steam, i.e. where the food is cooked in a steamer.

(b) By indirect contact, i.e. food is cooked between two plates over a pan of boiling water.

(c) In a basin inside a saucepan, which is one-third to a half full of boiling water, *or* half way up the side of the basin being used.

The water must be boiling before steaming starts and kept boiling right through the cooking period.

Allow half as long again in time for steaming as you would for boiling.

HERBS AND SPICES

HERBS

BASIL

There are several varieties of this herb, but I am concerned here with Common or Sweet Basil which is the most popular.

It's an annual plant and its leaves are similar in appearance to sage. When used in dishes which are to be cooked, use sparingly as the flavour increases when cooked.

It's widely used in French and Italian recipes and therefore a 'must' in tomato and sausage dishes. It can also be added with care to fish, cheese and egg dishes, mixed with other herbs in French Dressing and marinades, and a pinch on a salad gives it a nice flavour.

BAY LEAVES

These come from the true laurel tree and when dried have a strong flavour, so they should be used cautiously.

By adding just the right amount they can improve the flavouring of the following: soups, stews, sauces, salad dressings (i.e. oil and vinegar ones), fish, meat (i.e. roasting, marinading and when cooking bacon joints), poultry, game, rice and pasta dishes.

BOUQUET GARNI

This name is given to a small bunch of herbs, which in its simplest form contains a sprig of thyme, marjoram, a bay leaf and parsley, all of which are tied in a small muslin bag.

However, today it is easy to purchase BOUQUET GARNI in a tea-bag type sachet. In this case the spices have already been blended by the manufacturer and the sachets usually contain parsley, chervil, marjoram, thyme and bay leaf. One sachet put into a soup, casserole or marinade will enrich the flavour.

CHIVES

This herb is the smallest of the onion family, and has a mild flavour, so it can often be substituted for onion where this flavour is found to be too strong and the onion rather indigestible.

It grows from flat bulbs and has leaves rather like grass. The green leaves are the only part used in everyday cookery.

An obvious use is in salads, but because of its mild flavour it is also excellent combined with cream cheese, egg dishes, as a garnish for vegetables and potatoes instead of parsley. Mixed with butter it makes a nice accompaniment with grilled fish or meat, and is very good eaten with bread and butter.

DILL

An aromatic herb which has a fascinating flavour and is widely used almost all over the world. It improves the flavour of food and to some extent aids digestion, as in pickling cucumbers. It can also be used in the pickling of other vegetables.

The most common uses of this herb are in fish, soup, meat and salad dishes. It can also be used to flavour eggs and cream cheese, but on the whole it should be used with care.

MARJORAM

This herb has a strong sweet and spicy flavour and it should be used carefully, otherwise it can overpower the flavour of the dish being made. It improves all meat and poultry dishes, whether they be roasts or made-up dishes. When roasting, rub the meat with a little marjoram prior to cooking and notice the difference in the flavour. If the joint is to be stuffed, add some to the stuffing and don't rub the joint.

As it is a strong herb use sparingly in egg, cheese, soups and vegetable dishes.

ROSEMARY

A very fragrant herb which should be used with discretion. It's an evergreen shrub and the leaves are spiky, which makes them look rather like pine needles.

It can be used in the making of sweet dishes such as jellies and jams, and in savoury egg and cheese dishes. A few sprigs added when roasting lamb, beef, poultry and game give them a delicious flavour.

Used sparingly it also gives a subtle taste to fish.

SAGE

Use only first-class quality sage, as only then does it have a pungent flavour and should be used with discretion.

We all know the use of this herb with onion as a stuffing for pork and duck, but there are many more ways in which it can be used.

Here are a few examples: fish, liver, game, cream or cottage cheese, sausage dishes and soups.

If you are making a summer fruit drink a very little sage gives it a delicious flavour.

TARRAGON

This could almost be called the 'king' of herbs and it has a sweet and slightly bitter taste, so use it carefully otherwise it will spoil the dish. Considered in France of great importance in the making of classic sauces such as Bernaise and Hollandaise. It is also of prime importance in making a 'bouquet' of herbs.

Other uses are finely chopped in French Dressing or on green salads, garnishing vegetables which have a delicate flavour and in the cooking of meat, poultry, game and fish.

Do remember to use it sparingly otherwise the dish will be spoilt with the hidden 'tang'.

THYME

A very strong herb and therefore must only be used in small quantities. It is an essential ingredient of a BOUQUET GARNI and is used a great deal in fat meat dishes such as mutton and pork.

Other foods which can be improved in flavour by a small addition of this herb are shellfish, egg and cheese dishes, and in the stuffing of most poultry and game.

With regard to vegetables, blend a very little with some butter and toss the vegetables in it before serving. Suggested vegetables are carrots, asparagus, mushrooms, onions and potatoes.

SPICES
ALLSPICE

Called 'allspice' as its flavour is a mixture of several spices, i.e. cinnamon, nutmeg and cloves.

It is a berry and looks like a large brown peppercorn, but it should not be confused with mixed spice.

This spice can be bought whole or ground and is used mainly in stews, meat dishes, savouries and pickles, although it is sometimes recommended for use in the making of Christmas cakes and mincemeat.

CAPSICUM

Is the umbrella name for chillies and peppers of which there are several varieties. The red glossy pods are very hot in flavour and are used in the making of curries, chutneys and pickles. Dried and ground they become cayenne pepper or chilli powder.

The large red and green ones, which can be seen in most shops now, are used in salads, stews and rice dishes. If blanched and shredded before use they are easier on the digestion.

CARAWAY SEEDS

These are the seeds from the caraway plant which grows mainly in Europe. They are pungent and aromatic and are used to flavour cakes, biscuits and some types and varieties of bread and cheese.

CAYENNE PEPPER

This is prepared from the capsicum pepper and is therefore very hot, so use it carefully.

It is particularly good used in cheese dishes to bring out the flavour, and also in other savoury dishes.

Its colour is bright red and can be confused with paprika pepper which is almost the same colour.

CINNAMON

This can be purchased ground or in stick form and in the latter is useful for flavouring liquids used in puddings and sauces.

The ground variety is used mainly for flavouring cakes, stews and savoury dishes; also puddings, sauces and chutneys.

CLOVES

Some years ago I was in Zanzibar when the clove harvest was in progress and the smell from the dried flowerbuds was almost overpowering. They have a pungent flavour and can be bought whole or powdered.

The use of whole cloves when cooking bacon and ham is well known, as is the onion stuck with cloves that goes into the stewpot. When it comes to puddings and cakes I favour the powdered form, but use it very sparingly, so that it enhances the flavour and doesn't kill it.

CORIANDER SEED

These seeds have a pungent flavour and a slightly orange scent. Used in Indian and Arabic dishes and also highly spiced dishes such as curry, but do not add too much as the flavour is strong. This spice can be used in celery and fish dishes and in the stuffing for poultry.

Try rubbing a little on a piece of pork before roasting, it gives it a pleasant flavour.

It is usually bought in powdered form.

GINGER

There are three varieties – ground, crystallized and whole pickling (root). Ground ginger is used by people who find that sliced or chopped ginger is offensive in flavouring cakes and puddings. It is also used in some savoury dishes and is often served as an accompaniment to curry.

Crystallized is used, in the main, sliced or chopped in cakes, puddings and stewed fruit dishes, i.e. Rhubarb and Ginger.

Whole pickling (root) as its name implies, is used in the making of pickles. I also use it for making marrow and ginger preserves.

Before using it crush or bruise it to allow the flavour to come out and tie it in a small piece of muslin before adding it to the other ingredients.

MACE AND NUTMEG

I class these two together as mace is the outer shell or husk of the nutmeg and therefore they resemble each other in flavour.

Mace can be bought in blade form or ground and it is orange-yellow in colour. Nutmeg is bought whole or ground.

They are both used to flavour sweet and savoury sauces, cakes, puddings, stuffings, stews and potatoes. It is also traditional in Britain to grate it on top of milk puddings, junkets and custards.

Both of these spices should be used with discretion.

PAPRIKA

Made from pimentoes or sweet red peppers, it is an orange-red pepper and must not be confused with cayenne pepper.

Paprika has a mild flavour and is Hungarian in origin. It is used in making Hungarian Goulash and adds flavour and colour to a variety of dishes, either in the cooking or as a garnish.

VANILLA POD

It is a dried pod of an orchid, found in the tropics.

The pod can be used infused in milk or stored in a jar of sugar, once the pod has been removed from the sugar it can be used for making cakes requiring a vanilla flavour.

After use, rinse the pod, dry it thoroughly and then it is ready for use again. It can be used several times before the flavour finally disappears.

SOUPS

There's nothing like a home-made soup, whether it's made from fresh raw ingredients or from the left-over vegetables, because they're nourishing, full of flavour and you can season them to suit your family's taste.

In this section you'll find that I have included some good old fashioned recipes such as Beef Broth, Gran's Special Giblet Soup and Hot Potato Soup. The only changes I've made in these recipes is to shorten the time spent preparing them in the hope you'll try them.

Some of them are seasonal such as Broad Bean Soup, Leek Broth and Watercress Soup, but most of the others can be made all the year round.

BEEF BROTH

Ingredients

1¼ lb shin of beef
2 beef cubes
2 pints cold water
½ pint boiling water
2 carrots (peeled and diced)
1 small turnip (peeled and diced)
1 onion (peeled and diced)
1 leek (washed and diced)
1 oz pearl barley (washed)
salt and pepper
parsley (finely chopped)

METHOD
Remove the outer skin and any gristle from the beef and cut into small pieces.

Dissolve the cubes in the boiling water.

Put the meat, stock and cold water into a large saucepan and bring slowly to the boil. Skim the top if necessary and simmer gently for one hour.

In the meantime prepare the vegetables. After the hour's cooking add all the vegetables and barley and simmer for about 1 hour, when all the ingredients should be cooked, if not, allow a little longer. Before serving, check the seasoning and sprinkle with parsley.   (4–6 portions)

BROAD BEAN SOUP

Ingredients   **1 lb broad beans**
1 pint chicken stock
little thyme
1 teaspoonful arrowroot
¼ pint milk
1 oz butter
1 egg yolk
salt and pepper

METHOD
Boil the beans in the stock, with the thyme added for 20 minutes. Drain the beans, retaining the stock, and rub through a sieve or put in an electric blender. Return the sieved beans to the stock, season, and simmer for 10–15 minutes. Skim. Blend the arrowroot with milk and mix quickly in the pan, bring to the boil for 2 minutes, then add the butter in small pieces. Remove the pan from the heat. Blend a little soup with the egg yolk and then mix into the soup. Serve at once, garnished with extra beans.
(4 portions)

CHEESE SOUP

Ingredients   **1 onion (chopped)**
1 oz butter
1 oz plain flour
1 pint milk
½ pint water
2 tablespoonsful tomato purée
4 oz Cheddar cheese (grated)
salt and pepper

Fry the onion in the melted butter, mix in flour and cook for 2 minutes. Remove from the heat and add milk, water and tomato purée. Return the pan to the heat and simmer for 5 minutes. Remove from the heat again, add the cheese and seasonings. Serve with squares of toast or fried bread.

(4 portions)

CREAM OF CUCUMBER SOUP

Ingredients

1 pint white stock
1 small cucumber (peeled and cut into $\frac{1}{2}$ in. pieces)
1 teaspoonful shallot (chopped)
1 oz butter
$\frac{3}{4}$ oz plain flour
2 egg yolks
2·5 fl. oz milk
2·5 fl. oz real double dairy cream
salt and pepper

METHOD
Boil the stock, then add the cucumber and shallot and simmer for 15–20 minutes, or until they are soft, then rub through a sieve. Blend the butter and flour, cook together gently for a few minutes then add the sieved ingredients and stock. Stir well until it boils, then simmer for 5 minutes. Allow to cool then add the egg yolks, milk and cream and heat until the soup has thickened. Check seasoning before serving.   (4 portions)

FRESH VEGETABLE SOUP

Ingredients

2 oz butter
2 medium onions (peeled and sliced)
¾ lb carrots (peeled and sliced)
1 lb potatoes (peeled and sliced)
1 dessertspoonful sugar
salt and pepper
2½ pints stock
small pinch nutmeg
3 tablespoonsful single cream
little sherry (optional)

METHOD

Melt the butter in a large saucepan, add the onions and cook until soft but not coloured.

Add carrots, potatoes, sugar, salt and pepper and shake the pan well. Pour in the stock and cook all gently together until the vegetables are soft.

When cooked, rub the ingredients through a sieve or purée in a liquidiser. Return them to the saucepan, adjust the seasoning, add the nutmeg and re-heat.

Finally add the cream and sherry, just before serving but DO NOT BOIL. (4–6 portions)

GRAN'S SPECIAL GIBLET SOUP

Ingredients

2 sets giblets
2 oz butter
1 medium onion
1 large carrot
½ small head of celery
½ small savoy cabbage
½ turnip
bunch sweet herbs
salt
2 oz plain flour
2 quarts stock
½ teaspoonful peppercorns

Clean the giblets and blanch them. Put the butter in a saucepan with the sliced vegetables, salt and herbs, fry for 5 minutes, add flour, stock and giblets.

Bring to the boil, skim and simmer slowly for 2 hours. Pour through a fine sieve, return to the saucepan, reheat and serve. Serves about 8 portions, but this depends on the size of the soup-plates!

By the way, on special occasions, and if the purse-strings allowed, a glass of sherry went in just before the soup was served and it was garnished with chopped parsley.

HOT POTATO SOUP

Ingredients
$\frac{1}{2}$ lb peeled potatoes
1 medium-sized onion
1 pint stock or water
1 oz butter
salt and pepper
$\frac{1}{2}$ pint milk

METHOD

Grate the potatoes and onion, or put into an electric blender with some of the stock. Put the potatoes, onion stock or water, butter and seasonings into a saucepan, bring to the boil and simmer until the potato is tender, about 40–45 minutes.

Just before serving add the milk, reheat, and adjust the seasonings.

Serve piping hot, sprinkled with grated cheese, finely chopped parsley, grated nutmeg or paprika pepper. (4–6 portions)

LEEK BROTH

Ingredients
1 lb potatoes
2 carrots
small end of bacon (about 1 lb)
2 pints water
$\frac{1}{2}$ lb white cabbage
4 leeks
1 tablespoonful oatmeal
1 tablespoonful chopped parsley

Cut up the potatoes and carrots into small pieces and put them together with the bacon joint into a pan of boiling water. Boil for about 45 minutes to an hour or until tender. Remove the bacon and add the finely shredded cabbage and chopped leeks. Make the oatmeal into a paste with a little of the liquor and add for thickening. When cooked add the chopped parsley and serve. (4 portions)

SIMPLE MUSHROOM SOUP

Ingredients

8 oz mushrooms (finely sliced)
2 oz butter
1 large onion (finely sliced)
1 level tablespoonful cornflour
2 chicken cubes or 1½ pints chicken stock
½ pint milk
salt and pepper
little chopped parsley

METHOD
Gently fry the onions in the butter, until they look transparent, then add the mushrooms, stir together and cook for about 2 minutes. Blend the cornflour with a little cold water or stock, add the remainder of the stock and pour into the other ingredients. Cover the pan and simmer for 20 minutes.

When the soup is required add ½ pint milk and seasoning. Heat thoroughly, sprinkle with parsley when ready to serve. (4 portions)

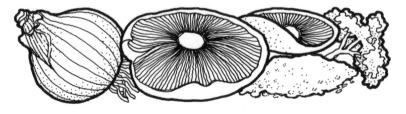

VEGETABLE SOUP

Ingredients

1 onion (sliced)
1 large carrot (sliced)
2 oz butter
1 tablespoonful plain flour
1½ lb tomatoes (sliced)
1½ pints stock
salt and pepper
1 teaspoonful sugar
bouquet garni

METHOD

Gently sauté the onion and carrot in 1 oz of butter. Then sprinkle the flour over the vegetables and brown them. Add the tomatoes and stock. Season to taste, add sugar and bouquet garni and simmer for 1 hour. Once all the ingredients are tender, pass them through a sieve, then reheat. Just before serving add the remainder of the butter. (4–6 portions)

WATERCRESS SOUP

Ingredients

4 bunches cultivated watercress
1 onion
1 teaspoonful celery salt
½ pint milk
1 oz butter
1½ pints lightly coloured stock
pepper to taste
pinch ground nutmeg

METHOD

Wash the cress and remove the stalks. Chop the onion. Put these into a saucepan with the celery salt, and cook in just sufficient water to stop them burning. When cooked, remove and rub through a sieve or pulverise in an electric liquidiser. Put the pulp back into the saucepan together with the milk, butter and stock and stir until it boils. Season, add nutmeg, and serve with croûtons. (4–6 portions)

MEAT (Main Course)

A question I'm often asked when shopping at the butchers is 'What can I give them for a change?' I realise just how difficult this is for housewives who have to produce at least one main meal a day, every day of the week and usually on a pretty tight budget.

With this in mind, I've compiled most of these recipes using the less expensive cuts of bacon, beef, pork and lamb. To help the meat go even further you'll find some of the joints are stuffed before they're roasted.

Most of the recipes indicate the number of portions for serving, but where the portions are not shown it is very much a question of how the joint is carved and the size of the portions served.

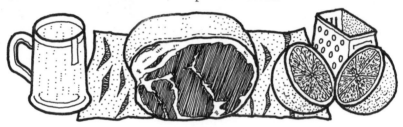

BACON COUNTRY STYLE

Ingredients
4 lb joint of collar bacon
¼ pint cider
1 large orange (grated rind and juice)

METHOD
Soak the joint in cold water overnight. Carefully remove the skin with a sharp knife. Lay the bacon on a piece of foil large enough to wrap it completely and place in a roasting pan. Turn the sides of the foil up, sprinkle with rind and juice of the orange and pour over the cider. Fold over the ends of the foil to form a parcel and press it together just to hold it in place. Bake at approximately 400°F (200°C) or Mark 6, allowing 25 minutes to the pound or approximately 2 hours cooking all together. Open up the foil when cooked and allow to become cold before carving. Serve with salad in season or hot vegetables and potatoes. (8–10 portions)

BAKED AND GLAZED FOREHOCK

Ingredients **4 lb boned and rolled forehock**
4 oz Demerara sugar
2 oz chopped blanched almonds
1 teaspoonful ground ginger
½ level teaspoonful dry mustard
small amount fresh orange juice

METHOD
Soak the bacon for several hours or overnight, dry with a cloth and score the rind. Lightly grease the base of the roasting pan and put joint in. Completely cover the joint with foil which has been well greased on the inside. Bake at 350°F (180°C) or Mark 4 for 1 hour 40 minutes, then take the joint from the oven, remove the rind and score the fat diagonally.

Prepare the glaze by mixing in a basin the sugar, almonds, ginger and mustard, until well blended, then add enough orange juice to bind to a paste. Spread this glaze over the fat of the joint and press well in. Return the joint to the oven at approximately 425°F (220°C) or Mark 7 for a further 20 minutes. Serve with roast potatoes and braised celery hearts.

(8–10 portions)

BEEF CASSEROLE

Ingredients **1 oz butter**
2–3 lb brisket of beef
1½ oz plain flour
salt and pepper
1 lb onions (sliced)
1 lb carrots (sliced)
1 lb tomatoes (skinned)
2 beef cubes dissolved in 1 pint boiling
  water
½ lb spaghetti
1 oz butter
3 oz grated Cheddar cheese

METHOD
Melt 1 oz of butter in a frying pan. Coat the meat in the flour to which has been added a little salt and pepper, then brown the joint all over in the

melted butter. Put the onions, carrots, and tomatoes into a deep ovenproof casserole, place the joint on top and add the stock.

Cover the casserole with a well-fitting lid and cook at approximately 300°F (150°C) or Mark 2 for about 3½ hours.

Shortly before the joint has finished cooking, cook the spaghetti, drain well and toss in 1 oz of melted butter and the finely grated cheese.

Serve the brisket on top of the sphaghetti, and garnish with the vegetables. (4–6 portions)

BRAISED BRISKET OF BEEF

Ingredients
½ head celery
1 oz butter or dripping
2 lb boned and rolled brisket
1 large piece bacon rind
½ lb onions (sliced)
½ lb carrots (cut in quarters)
½ level teaspoonful salt
¼ level teaspoonful pepper
½ pint red wine or meat stock

METHOD

Wash and cut the celery into 1½ in. lengths. Melt the fat in an ovenproof casserole and fry the meat until it is brown all over. Remove the meat, place the bacon rind at the bottom of the casserole, add the vegetables and lastly the meat on top. Add the seasonings and wine or stock then put on the lid. Cook gently until the meat is tender at approximately 350°F (180°C) or Mark 4 for about 2½–3 hours.

N.B. This dish can be served as a joint or sliced. Suggested vegetables, peas, green beans, or spinach with new or mashed potatoes.

(4 portions)

CROWN ROAST OF LAMB

Ingredients   3½ lb best neck of lamb, prepared for a crown
                  roast
                  STUFFING
                  8 oz fresh white breadcrumbs
                  4 oz chopped suet
                  2 tablespoonsful chopped parsley
                  1 teaspoonful dried herbs
                  rind of 1 lemon (grated)
                  2 eggs
                  1 chopped kidney
                  salt and pepper to taste

METHOD

Make the stuffing by putting all the ingredients into a basin, except the eggs. Beat the eggs lightly, add to the other ingredients and bind the stuffing together. Place the stuffing in the centre of the two sections of neck, then skewer and tie them together with string, this will pull them into a crown shape. Twist some pieces of butter paper or aluminium foil round each of the exposed bones, and roast at approximately 350°F (180°C) or Mark 4. Allow 30 minutes to the lb plus a further 30 minutes.

Serve with cutlet frills on the ends of the bones, piped potatoes and watercress or parsley round the base of the dish, and garnish with a slice of tomato between each bone.   (5–6 portions)

FAMILY CASSEROLE

Ingredients   1 lb stewing steak (cut into ½ in. cubes)
                  1 oz plain flour⎱
                  salt and pepper⎰seasoned flour
                  1½ oz butter
                  2 medium sized carrots (sliced)
                  2 medium sized onions (sliced)
                  ½ in. sliced parsnip OR turnip (diced)
                  10½ oz can condensed mushroom soup mixed
                    with 1 can water

METHOD

Have ready a 2½ pint ovenproof casserole with a well-fitting lid. Toss the meat in the seasoned flour. Melt the butter in a frying pan, add the meat and fry until brown all over, then put the meat into the casserole.

Add the carrots, onions and turnip or parsnip to the casserole. Pour over the soup and water which have been mixed together. Cover with the lid and cook at approximately 350°F (180°C) or Mark 4 for 2½–3 hours, or until the meat is tender.

This dish is very nice served with:
(a) Hot boiled rice
(b) Plain or herb dumplings
(c) Mashed, boiled or jacket potatoes

(4 portions)

FARMHOUSE HAND OF PORK

Ingredients
1 hand of pork
3 new carrots
2 small onions
2 courgettes (baby marrows)
½ pint water
salt and pepper
1 teaspoonful Demerara sugar
¼ teaspoonful thyme

METHOD
Rub the rind of the pork with the seasoning and thyme. Place the joint into a casserole, add the sugar and water and cover with a well-fitting lid. Bake in the oven at approximately 425°F (220°C) or Mark 6 for 20 minutes. Remove the lid, add the roughly chopped vegetables, cover and cook for a further 1½ hours at approximately 375°F (190°C) or Mark 5.

Serve with new potatoes and buttered leaf spinach, using the liquor as the sauce.

(6–8 portions)

GAMMON SLIPPER

Ingredients
1½–2 lb gammon slipper
2 small onions
bay leaf
1 teaspoonful soft brown sugar (pieces)
small quantity coarse oatmeal

METHOD

Soak the joint for 6 hours or overnight if preferred. Rub the sugar into the meat section of the joint and leave for 20 minutes. Into a saucepan put the joint, onions, bay leaf and enough water to cover the joint, then bring slowly almost to boiling point. Remove any scum as it rises, reduce the heat to simmering point, and simmer 25 minutes to the pound. Twenty minutes before the cooking time is completed, take the joint from the saucepan, remove the skin and coat the fat with coarse oatmeal, pressing it well into the fat. Put into an oven, at approximately 425°F (220°C) or Mark 7 until the oatmeal is golden brown – about 30 minutes.

(3–4 portions)

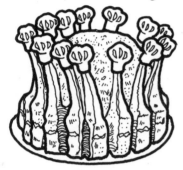 

HALF CROWN ROAST OF LAMB

Ingredients

1½ lb best neck of lamb (chined)
dripping or butter for roasting
small tin pineapple rings
small quantity redcurrant jelly

METHOD

Mix a little redcurrant jelly with the butter or dripping and spread over the joint. Cover the ends of the bones with foil or greaseproof paper to save them burning. Put the joint in the roasting pan and roast at approximately 350°F (180°C) or Mark 4. Allow 30 minutes to the pound, plus a further 30 minutes.

Just before the joint is cooked, place the pineapple rings in a lightly buttered dish or grill pan and heat through.

When cooked remove the paper from the ends of the bones, and put one cutlet frill on each, before serving with the pineapple.

Suggested vegetables to serve with the dish: roast parsnips, which can be done round the joint. Braised carrots, cooked in a casserole in the oven and either roast or jacket potatoes.

(3 portions)

KNUCKLE OF PORK AND PEASE PUDDING

Ingredients

1 knuckle of pork (approximately 1½ lb)
1 pint water
1½ lb sauerkraut
1 medium-sized potato (grated)
pinch caster sugar
salt to taste

METHOD

Into a saucepan put the water and knuckle of pork, bring them to the boil and simmer for approximately 1½ hours. Remove the knuckle from the pan, add the sauerkraut and replace the knuckle on top. Bring the ingredients to the boil again and then simmer for a further hour.

Remove the knuckle and sauerkraut, and place on a heated serving dish.

Thicken the liquid in the saucepan with the potato, bring to the boil, season with salt and sugar and serve.

Traditional accompaniments to be eaten with this dish are boiled potatoes and pease pudding. (4 portions)

PEASE PUDDING

Ingredients

½ lb split peas
1 oz butter
1 egg
pepper and salt
pinch sugar

METHOD

Wash the peas well, and soak in water overnight.

The following day tie them loosely in a pudding cloth (this allows for swelling). Put into a pan of boiling water, and boil for approximately 3–4 hours until the peas are quite soft.

Allow them to drain very well, before rubbing them through a wire sieve or colander. Add the butter, well-beaten egg, pepper, salt and sugar, and beat well for a few minutes until thoroughly mixed.

Return the pudding to the cloth, tie up tightly and boil for approximately 20 minutes. Turn the pudding out on to a serving dish, serving it round the knuckle. (4 portions)

Hot potato soup, p. 39; whole melon delight, p. 138; barbecued chicken grill, p. 66; prawn salad with hot mayonnaise, p. 88.

MARMALADE GLAZED LAMB

Ingredients

$\frac{1}{2}$ or whole shoulder of lamb (boned, rolled
   and tied)
salt and pepper to season meat
3 tablespoonsful orange marmalade
1 tablespoonful fresh lemon juice
1 tablespoonful parsley (finely chopped)
little salt and pepper

METHOD

Season the joint with salt and pepper, and roast in the normal way until
there is 15 minutes left for cooking.

While the meat is cooking make the glaze by blending 1 teaspoonful of
salt, $\frac{1}{2}$ teaspoonful of pepper with the marmalade, lemon juice and
parsley.

Now drain the fat from the roasting pan, put the glaze on top of the
meat and baste frequently during the remaining cooking time.

(4–8 portions)

MIDDLE GAMMON WITH ORANGE GLAZE

Ingredients

1 piece middle gammon approximately $4\frac{1}{2}$ lb
1 bay leaf
1 blade mace

GLAZE
4 oz Demerara sugar
2 oranges
approximately 18 cloves

METHOD

Soak the joint for 6 hours or overnight if preferred. Put the joint into a
saucepan with the bay leaf and blade of mace, and cover the joint with
water. Bring slowly to almost boiling point, remove any scum as it rises,
and reduce the heat to simmering point and simmer 25 minutes to the lb.
Take the joint from the saucepan, remove the skin and place in a greased
roasting pan. Score the fat diagonally and spread the glaze on; then cut
the second orange into slices and place on the glaze; stud the centre of
each slice with 3 cloves and put the joint into the oven at approx. 425°F

49

Pork and potato hotpot, p. 50; minted chops, p. 50; bacon country style, p. 42.

(220°C) or Mark 7 for 25 minutes. Served hot or cold this joint is delicious.
TO MAKE THE GLAZE While the joint is cooking put the sugar, grated rind of one orange and sufficient juice to form a paste into a basin. Use as directed above.   (8–10 portions)

MINTED CHOPS

Ingredients
**4 English loin of lamb chops
2 level tablespoonsful parsley (chopped)
1 level tablespoonful mint (chopped)
1 oz butter
salt and pepper to taste**

METHOD
Trim any excess fat from the chops then make a slit right through each chop at the side of the bone.

In a basin mix well together all the other ingredients and when evenly blended, put the stuffing into the slits.

Place each chop in the base of the grill pan and grill for approximately 15–20 minutes turning them over once during the cooking period.
Suggested vegetables to serve with the above chops:
1. Mashed potatoes which have been piped on to a baking sheet, brushed with a little milk and browned under the grill.
2. Buttered cucumber, i.e. ½ cucumber peeled and cut into thick slices, which are cooked in 1½ oz of butter until tender, but not broken.

(4 portions)

PORK AND POTATO HOT-POT

Ingredients
**1 lb diced shoulder of pork
seasoned flour
½ lb sliced onions
little dripping for frying
½ lb sliced, skinned tomatoes OR 1 large can
    tomatoes
salt and pepper to taste
1½ lb peeled and sliced potatoes
approx. ½ pint stock or cider**

Coat the pork in a little seasoned flour and fry with the onions in a little dripping, until the meat has browned all over and the onions are opaque. Put half of this mixture into a deep ovenproof casserole. Add half the tomatoes and potatoes in layers, seasoning as you go. Continue adding the ingredients in layers until they are all used, ending with a layer of potatoes. Dot the potatoes with a little dripping, add the stock or cider to come two-thirds up the casserole and cover with a well-fitting lid. Bake for $1\frac{1}{2}$–2 hours at approximately 325°F (160°C) or Mark 3.

Remove the lid about 20 minutes before serving to brown the potatoes on the top. (4 portions)

ROAST STUFFED BREAST OF LAMB

Ingredients

1 breast of lamb
4 oz liver (lamb's for preference)
2 rashers of bacon
1 medium-sized onion (finely chopped)
$\frac{1}{2}$ oz butter
2 oz fresh white breadcrumbs
1 level teaspoonful dried mixed herbs
1 small orange (grated rind and juice)
salt and pepper
little stock

METHOD

Remove all the bones from the lamb, or ask the butcher to do this. Place the lamb skin side down and season well with salt and pepper. Wash the liver and dry well. In a frying pan, gently cook the bacon until the fat runs. Remove the bacon, add the butter and fry the liver for about 4 minutes on each side. Remove the liver and add the onion and fry until golden brown.

Mince the liver and bacon and put into a bowl with the onion, bread-crumbs, herbs, orange rind and juice, add sufficient stock to bind the ingredients together and mix well. Season with a little salt and pepper if required. Spread the stuffing on the inside of the lamb, roll up and secure with string. Roast at approximately 375°F (190°C) or Mark 5 for about $1\frac{1}{4}$ hours. Serve hot or cold. (3 portions)

ROAST STUFFED SHOULDER OF LAMB

Ingredients   1 × 5¼ lb boned shoulder of lamb

STUFFING
2 oz butter
3½ oz fresh breadcrumbs
2 tablespoonsful finely chopped mixed herbs
2 medium sized onions (finely chopped)
2 oranges (grated rind only)
1 tablespoonful orange juice
2 eggs (beaten)

METHOD
Melt the butter and gently fry the onion. Put the breadcrumbs, herbs and fried onions into a basin, and mix with the orange rind, juice and beaten eggs, until blended.

Wipe the shoulder of lamb, spread the stuffing evenly on the inside of the meat. Roll up and tie with string. Put in a roasting pan and roast for about 2¼ hours at approximately 350°F (180°C) or Mark 4.

STUFFED BEST NECK OF LAMB

Ingredients   1½ lb best neck of lamb, prepared for stuffing

STUFFING
4 oz fresh white breadcrumbs
2 oz chopped suet
1 tablespoonful chopped mint
1 teaspoonful dried herbs (optional)
little grated lemon rind
1 egg
salt and pepper to taste

METHOD
Make the stuffing by putting all the ingredients into a basin, except the egg. Beat the egg lightly, add to the other ingredients and bind the stuffing together. Place the stuffing on the inside of the meat, roll up and secure with skewers or string. Roast at approximately 350°F (180°C) or Mark 4. Allow 30 minutes to the pound plus a further 30 minutes.   (3 portions)

STUFFED STREAKY PORK

Ingredients
$2\frac{1}{2}$ lb boned and scored streaky pork
4 oz pork sausage meat
2 oz fresh white breadcrumbs
1 small onion (finely chopped)
$\frac{1}{4}$ teaspoonful dried sage
$\frac{1}{4}$ teaspoonful dried thyme
1 level dessertspoonful chopped parsley
pepper and salt
mustard
1 egg

METHOD
Wipe the joint with a clean damp cloth, spread some ready-mixed English
mustard on the inside of the meat. Make the stuffing by mixing together
all the remaining ingredients until evenly blended, then spread over the
joint on top of the mustard. Roll up the joint and secure well with string.
Rub the scored rind with some common block salt so that it gets well into
the score marks. Place in a roasting pan and roast at approximately 400°F
(200°C) or Mark 6 for about 2 hours. Serve either hot or cold.

(4–6 portions)

WAGON WHEEL OF LAMB

Ingredients
best end of lamb (chopped NOT chined)
little fat for roasting
4 slices pineapple
$\frac{1}{2}$ oz soft brown sugar
juice $\frac{1}{2}$ lemon
8 oz pasta (Wagon Wheels)
2 oz butter
few sprigs parsley

METHOD
Make a slit in the lamb between each chop, long enough to take a half
slice of pineapple.

Cut the pineapple slices in half and insert one piece into each slit. Place
the joint in a roasting pan, and add sufficient fat for roasting the joint,
cover with a piece of foil and cook at approximately 425°F (220°C) or

Mark 7 allowing 25 minutes to the pound and 25 minutes over. Half an hour before the cooking time is completed, remove the foil to allow the joint and pineapple to brown. When cooked, put on to a hot serving dish.

Cook the pasta as instructed on the packet, then toss in the 2 oz butter. Pour off the surplus fat from the roasting tin and add the pineapple juice, lemon juice and sugar, cook over a medium heat, stirring well to ensure an even blending of the ingredients, when the liquid has reduced slightly pour into a heated sauce boat. Garnish the dish with the parsley and serve.

(5–6 portions)

ZENA'S STEAK AND KIDNEY PIE

Ingredients

$\frac{1}{2}$ **lb rough puff pastry**
1$\frac{1}{2}$ lb skirt or chuck and blade beef
$\frac{1}{4}$ **lb ox kidney**
1 oz plain flour
salt and pepper
cold water

METHOD

Cut the meat into small cubes, remove the core from the kidney and cut likewise. Toss both in the flour which has been seasoned with salt and pepper. Put into a saucepan and add sufficient cold water to just cover the meat. Cook very slowly until the meat is tender. Turn into a 1$\frac{1}{2}$-pint pie dish which is ovenproof, placing a funnel in the centre if desired.

Cover with the pastry rolled out to size.

Place on a baking sheet and bake at approximately 425°F (220°C) or Mark 7 for about 45 minutes or until the pastry is a rich golden brown.

(4 portions)

MEAT (Miscellaneous)

As the heading of this section implies, this is a miscellany of meat dishes and here you'll find recipes for stews, casseroles, mince, liver and brawn.

Most of them are what I would suggest for mid-week meals as on the whole they're quick and easy to prepare and won't stretch the purse strings too far.

On the other hand New Zealand Ragout, Bacon Grill or Beef Olives could be useful when entertaining, but if you want a cold main course then Apple and Pork Loaf or Ham and Egg Mould could be the ones for you as they can be made in advance.

APPLE AND PORK LOAF

Ingredients
    1 lb minced raw pork
    4 oz rolled oats
    $\frac{3}{4}$ pint sieved apples (cooked)
    1 egg
    1 teaspoonful mixed herbs
    $\frac{1}{2}$ teaspoonful Tabasco sauce

METHOD
In a basin mix all the ingredients well together until evenly blended. Press these ingredients well down into a $1\frac{1}{2}$ lb greased loaf tin, or similar tin. Cover tightly and bake about $1\frac{1}{4}$ hours at 350°F (180°C) or Mark 4.

This loaf can be steamed if preferred.

When cooked turn out on to a serving dish and serve hot with a tomato sauce.

If preferred cold – allow to become quite cold before glazing with aspic, in this case set some slices of an unpeeled eating apple down the centre.   (4 portions)

BACONBURGERS

Ingredients
    1 lb lean bacon (finely minced)
    1 onion (finely minced)
    small pinch mixed herbs
    1 small teaspoonful mixed mustard

METHOD

Put the bacon and onion into a basin, add the herbs and mustard and mix well. Divide the mixture into 6 equal portions and mould into flat cakes, with floured hands. Fry in shallow fat for about 5 minutes, turning once. Serve in toasted or plain buttered baps, put one baconburgher into each bap, and top with a slice of cheese, and grill until the cheese melts.

N.B. This filling can also be cooked in the oven. To do this hollow out 6 bread rolls, put the filling in the hollows and bake at approx. 375°F (190°C) or Mark 5 for about 20 minutes.   (6 portions)

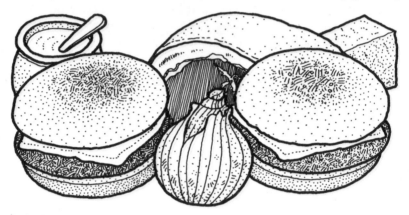

BACON GRILL

Ingredients

4 chops of collar bacon cut ½ in. thick
4 tomatoes
1 small can pineapple rings
1 oz butter
salt and pepper
small quantity of Demerara sugar

METHOD

Remove the rind from the bacon and snip the fat at ½ in. intervals, place them in the grill pan and pour over the pineapple juice. Season and dot with the butter.

Place them under a hot grill to seal on both sides, and continue grilling until cooked.

Three to four minutes before the cooking is completed, add the tomatoes and pineapple rings which have been sprinkled with sugar.

Serve immediately they are cooked.   (4 portions)

BACON RISSOTTO

Ingredients
**8 oz cooked collar bacon
2 oz butter
1 medium sized onion (finely chopped)
1 green pepper
3 oz patna rice
1 pint chicken stock
3 oz fresh mushrooms (sliced)
2 large tomatoes (skinned and chopped)
small packet frozen peas
pimento**

METHOD
Cut the cold bacon into $\frac{1}{2}$ in. cubes.

Melt the butter in a saucepan and lightly fry the onion for a few minutes. Cut the pepper in half and remove the seeds, then cut it into thin strips and add to the onion. Add the rice and fry all together gently for 2–3 minutes, stirring from time to time.

Add the stock and simmer for 10 minutes. Then add the bacon, mushrooms, skinned and chopped tomatoes and peas and cook for a further 10 minutes, or until the ingredients are thoroughly heated through.

Serve piled up in the centre of a hot dish and garnish with thin strips of pimento.   (3–4 portions)

BEEF CASSEROLE

Ingredients
**1 oz butter
1½ lb shin of beef (cut into cubes)
10½ oz can condensed cream of celery soup
¼ pint water
4 oz mushrooms (sliced)
1 large onion (sliced)
1 rounded tablespoonful chopped gherkins or
  sour cucumbers**

METHOD
Melt the butter in a frying pan, and fry the beef gently for about 3 minutes. Put it into an ovenproof casserole and add all remaining ingredients. Cover with a lid and bake at approximately 350°F (180°C) or Mark 4 for about 2 hours or until the meat is tender.   (4–6 portions)

BEEF OLIVES

Ingredients

1 lb buttock steak
1 oz butter or dripping
½ pint stock
2 oz chopped and fried mushrooms
salt and pepper
little flour
4–6 oz veal forcemeat
mashed potatoes
few sprigs of parsley

METHOD

Remove skin and fat from the meat, and wipe with a damp cloth. Cut into small oblong pieces as near the same size as possible. Beat them out slightly with a rolling pin or butter pat. Spread a little stuffing onto each piece and roll up, then tie them like a parcel with fine string, and coat with flour. Put them into a pan in which you have melted the fat, and brown them all over. Lift them out onto a plate and pour off the fat. To the same pan add the stock, seasonings and mushrooms, and when hot add the rolls, and simmer very gently until the meat is tender, about 1 hour.

TO SERVE Lift the beef olives onto a hot plate and remove the string. Arrange in a pattern on mashed potatoes, and decorate with parsley. Green peas or carrots are suggested as the vegetables with this dish.

(3–4 portions)

BRAIN AND KIDNEY PATTIES

Ingredients

brains
2 lamb's kidneys
1 tablespoonful vinegar
4 level tablespoonsful breadcrumbs
1 teaspoonful finely chopped parsley
1 teaspoonful dried thyme
salt and pepper
1 egg
1 oz dripping

METHOD

Wash the brains with the vinegar and 1 pint of cold water. Boil with the kidneys in this liquid for 10 minutes. Drain and chop them. Put them into a basin and mix together with the breadcrumbs, parsley, thyme, pepper and salt and beaten egg. Heat the dripping in a frying-pan, drop spoonfuls of the mixture into the pan and fry until golden-brown. Serve hot with a salad. (2–3 portions)

EASY LAMB STEW

Ingredients

1 lb scrag of lamb (cut into pieces)
little seasoned flour
1 oz dripping or lard
$\frac{3}{4}$ pint stock or water
$\frac{1}{4}$ lb carrots
3 small onions
3 small tomatoes

METHOD

Trim the meat, removing any excess fat. Prepare the vegetables. Toss the meat in the seasoned flour, and shake off any surplus. Heat the fat in a frying pan, add the meat and brown slightly. Transfer the meat to a deep ovenproof casserole, add stock, carrots and onions. Cover with a lid and cook at approximately 325°F (160°C) or Mark 3 for about 2 hours.

Remove from the oven, correct the seasoning and add the tomatoes. Continue cooking for a further 30 minutes at the same temperature or until the meat and vegetables are tender. Serve with potatoes.

(3–4 portions)

HAMBURGER CASSEROLE

Ingredients

8 small onions or shallots
1 lb minced beef
2½ oz fresh breadcrumbs
pinch salt and pepper
small pinch mixed herbs
1 egg (lightly beaten)
1 can condensed tomato soup
finely chopped parsley (to garnish)

METHOD

Cook the onions until tender and drain. Mix together the beef, bread-crumbs, seasonings, and bind with the egg. Divide the mixture into 8 equal portions and shape into balls. Make a depression in the centre of each one and press in an onion. Put the meat balls into a greased oven-proof dish, spoon the soup over the meat and bake, closely covered for about 30 minutes at approx. 350°F (180°C) or Mark 4. Sprinkle with parsley before serving.   (4 portions)

HAM AND EGG MOULD

Ingredients

1 pint aspic jelly
2 hard-boiled eggs
4 stuffed olives (chopped)
3–4 gherkins (chopped)
4–6 oz diced cooked ham
watercress and tomatoes for garnishing

METHOD

Melt the aspic as directed on the packet. Pour into a ring mould enough jelly to give a layer about ¼ in. in depth. Allow this to become firm but not too set, then arrange slices of hard-boiled egg and halved stuffed olives to form a design. Chill to set the decoration, then spoon on some more aspic to cover the decoration. While this is setting add all the other ingredients to the remaining jelly, and stir until evenly blended. Pour this mixture gently into the mould and allow to set firm.
TO SERVE Turn the jelly out of the mould and garnish with watercress and tomatoes.   (4–6 portions)

LIVER CASSEROLE

Ingredients

1 lb liver
small quantity of plain flour
salt and pepper
2 oz butter or dripping
½ lb onions (sliced)
½ pint stock
1 lb potatoes
1 lb swedes

METHOD

Wash, trim and slice the liver. Roll in seasoned flour and fry in 1 oz of butter or dripping, with the onions, until lightly browned.

Place the ingredients in a casserole, add the stock and cook gently for about 1¼ hours, at approximately 350°F (180°C) or Mark 4.

In the meantime boil the potatoes and swedes until tender, drain and mash them either together or separately, adding a little butter, pepper and salt. Serve very hot.   (4 portions)

NEW ZEALAND RAGOUT

Ingredients

1 oz butter
1 small onion (peeled and chopped)
¼ level teaspoonful ground ginger
1 can condensed tomato soup
½ can water
1 teaspoonful Worcester sauce
1 bay leaf
pinch mixed spice
2 level tablespoonsful clear honey
1–1½ lb lean lamb (cubed)
2 oz plain flour
4 oz blackcurrants (fresh, frozen or canned)

METHOD

Melt the butter in a frying pan, add onion and ginger and fry until golden brown. Add tomato soup, water, sauce, bay leaf, spice and honey. Bring the ingredients to the boil, stirring all together, and strain.

Toss the meat in the flour and fry in a little butter for a few minutes.

Put the sauce and meat into a casserole and add the blackcurrants. Cook at approx. 350°F (180°C) or Mark 4 for 1½–2 hours.

N.B. VERY IMPORTANT If frozen or canned blackcurrants are used, allow them to thaw if frozen, and drain off all surplus juice before adding the currants to the casserole. (8 portions)

PIG'S HEAD BRAWN

Ingredients

**1 pig's head
2 handsful of cooking salt
1 small piece of saltpetre
water
3 carrots
3 turnips
½ lb onions
bunch of herbs
3 peppercorns
3 cloves
2 blades of mace
1 bay leaf**

METHOD

Thoroughly wash and clean the head. Put it into brine all night OR sprinkle with cooking salt and saltpetre. Rinse it well before putting it into a heavy pan.

Cover with cold water and boil for 2–3 hours, or until the meat leaves the bones easily. Skin the ears and tongue and dice the meat, returning the bones to the liquor.

Bring to the boil then add the vegetables (roughly chopped) and seasoning.

Boil for at least 1 hour until the stock has greatly reduced.

There should now be about 1½ pints of liquor. Strain the liquor into another pan. Put the meat into the pan, season again to taste, and bring to the boil.

Rinse a mould or basin in cold water before pouring in the meat and liquor.

When the brawn has set it is excellent with a spring onion, cucumber and tomato salad. (8–10 portions)

PORK AND MUSHROOM CASSEROLE

Ingredients
$1\frac{1}{4}$ lb blade of pork
1 egg
1 onion
4 oz mushrooms
4 rashers streaky bacon
approx. 1 pint stock
small quantity browned breadcrumbs
small quantity of butter
salt and pepper

METHOD
Remove the rind from the meat, and also some of the fat. Cut the bacon into small pieces and fry until the fat runs. Put the bacon onto a plate, and into the frying pan add the chopped onion, mushrooms, a small knob of butter and cook gently for a few minutes. Remove these from the pan and add the pork which has been cut into small pieces and coated in egg and breadcrumbs; fry quickly until golden brown. Place all ingredients in layers into a large casserole, season, add sufficient stock to cover and put the lid on. Bake at approx. 350°F (180°C) or Mark 4 for about 2 hours.   (4 portions)

PORK STEW WITH DUMPLINGS

Ingredients
STEW
$3-3\frac{1}{2}$ lb hock of pork
2 large onions
3–4 large carrots
1 small swede or turnip
salt and pepper
stock made from the bones

DUMPLINGS
5 oz self-raising flour
1 oz lard
2 oz chopped suet
1 egg
pinch salt

METHOD

Get the butcher to saw the hock into 4 pieces, then remove all bones and put on to cook with water to cover them. Trim the skin and any surplus fat from the meat and cut into cubes. Put the meat into a large saucepan and cover with stock, simmer for 45 minutes before adding the vegetables. Prepare the vegetables and cut all of them into quarters, add to the saucepan and season to taste. Continue cooking slowly until tender.

In the meantime in a basin rub the lard into the flour, add salt and suet and bind together with the beaten egg. Shape into small dumplings, bring the stew to the boil and drop them in 15 minutes before serving.

(4–6 portions)

RINGED LAMB CHOPS

Ingredients
**3 loin chops
2 lamb's kidneys
3 rashers bacon
2 oz dripping**

METHOD

Trim the excess fat from the chops. Skin the kidneys and halve them, taking out the white cores. Take the bones out of the chops, and curl each one round half a kidney. Wrap a piece of bacon round the chops and fix in place with a skewer. Fry very gently in the dripping until cooked through, turning during cooking.

(3 portions)

SAUSAGE IN A NUTSHELL

Ingredients
**1 lb pork sausage meat
6 oz cooked mashed potatoes
1 teaspoonful sage (finely chopped)
salt and pepper
little seasoned flour
1 beaten egg
3 oz finely chopped walnuts**

METHOD

In a basin mix sausage meat, potatoes, sage and seasoning; when evenly blended divide the mixture into 8 equal portions. With floured hands shape each portion into a flat disc about 3 in. in diameter. Dip into the

64

Apple and pork loaf, p. 55; sausage in a nutshell, p. 64; beef olives, p. 58.

egg and cover all over with walnuts. Place on the grill-pan grid and cook under a medium heat for 10 minutes, turning them about twice during cooking. These are delicious served with apple sauce. (8 portions)

SPRING LAMB WITH WATERCRESS SAUCE

Ingredients

4 neck end lamb chops
2 oz butter
2 bunches watercress
½ lb onions
¾ lb potatoes
½ pint chicken stock
1 level teaspoonful sage
1 bay leaf
salt and pepper to taste
3 tablespoonsful double dairy cream

METHOD
Chop the potatoes and onions into chunks, and put them into a large saucepan together with the watercress, which has been roughly cut up with scissors. Add chicken stock, seasoning, and herbs and simmer until tender. Remove the bay leaf, then rub the remaining ingredients through a sieve or pulverize in an electric blender, and adjust the seasoning. Meanwhile trim the chops, removing any excess fat and seal in hot butter. Transfer the chops to an ovenproof casserole and pour the sauce over. Cook at 325°F (160°C) or Mark 3 for 2-2½ hours until the chops are tender.

TO SERVE Remove the chops from the casserole, and put into a hot serving dish, stir the cream into the sauce in the casserole and pour over the chops. (4 portions)

Gazpacho, p. 98; mushroom pudding, p. 99; Emett baked potato special, p. 98.

POULTRY & GAME

Most of the recipes in this section are devoted to chicken, which is a popular and economical buy when feeding the family. At the same time, oven-ready birds don't seem to have the flavour of a fresh chicken as far as I am concerned, so it's necessary to cook and serve them with the addition of other ingredients to make them really tasty.

Here you'll find recipes which use whole chicken, half chicken, joints and even the left-overs and we still have the carcass left to make the stock for home-made soup.

Duck and Goose are also included as they're full of flavour, not nearly as fatty as they used to be and have a delicious crisp skin when roasted. Finally, I've included Stuffed Turkey and Mother's Jugged Hare, so there should be something for everyone.

BARBECUED CHICKEN GRILL

Ingredients

1 chicken 2–2½ lb in weight OR
2 chicken halves of the same weight
2 oz butter or margarine
4 tablespoonsful malt vinegar
1 tablespoonful Worcester sauce
1 tablespoonful tomato purée
1 level tablespoonful Demerara sugar
1 teaspoonful onion (finely grated)
1 teaspoonful paprika
½ teaspoonful salt
little watercress to garnish

METHOD

Divide the chicken in half through the breastbone and backbone. Skewer each half as flat as possible. Melt the butter in a small saucepan and brush liberally over the chicken. Put the chicken skin side down in the base of the grill pan, and cook gently 5–6 inches below the heat for 12–15 minutes. Meanwhile add the remaining ingredients to the butter in the saucepan and simmer together for 2 minutes. Turn the chicken over, brush with the barbecue sauce and continue grilling gently for a further 12–15 minutes or until the joints move freely.

TO SERVE Pour the remaining sauce over the chicken and garnish the dish with the watercress.   (4 portions)

CELERY CHICKEN

Ingredients
3–4 chicken portions
1 oz butter
10½ oz can condensed cream of celery soup
little chopped parsley
¼ pint milk (approximately ½ a can)
1 dessertspoonful fresh lemon juice
seasoning to taste

METHOD
Melt the butter in a large, deep ovenproof dish. Wipe the chicken portions and place skin side down in the dish, and pour over the lemon juice. Bake at approximately 400°F (200°C) or Mark 6 for 20 minutes, then turn the chicken over and bake a further 30–40 minutes at the same temperature.

Stir the milk into the condensed soup, season to taste, and pour over the chicken joints, sprinkle the top with parsley and bake a further 20 minutes covered with a piece of foil. Serve with potatoes baked in their jackets.
                                                                      (3–4 portions)

CHICKEN AND WATERCRESS POT-ROAST

Ingredients
2 oz dripping
2 onions
4 carrots
1 swede
2 bay leaves
3 lb chicken
salt and pepper
1 oz butter
1 oz flour
1 bunch watercress

METHOD
Heat the dripping then turn the sliced onions, carrots and swede into the pan and stir them together for a few minutes. Add the bay leaves, whole

chicken and enough water to half-cover the bird. Add seasoning then simmer gently until tender, basting the breast from time to time. When cooked blend the butter and flour with 1 pint of the stock, add the chopped watercress and bring to the boil, stirring from time to time. Pour over the chicken and serve. (4 portions)

CHICKEN, CELERY AND APPLE SALAD

Ingredients
4 level tablespoonsful mayonnaise
4 level tablespoonsful top of the milk
approx. $\frac{1}{2}$ level teaspoonful salt
2 large dessert apples (cored and cut into dice)
4–5 sticks celery (sliced)
8 oz cooked chicken (cut into dice)
little finely chopped walnut
1 large tomato
few lettuce leaves

METHOD
In a large basin mix together the mayonnaise, top of the milk and salt. Add the apple, celery and chicken and stir until evenly blended. If possible allow the mixture to stand in a cool place for about an hour, as this will allow the flavours to blend together.

Arrange the lettuce on a serving dish, pile the mixture in the centre, sprinkle with the chopped walnuts and garnish with tomato.

(3–4 portions)

CHICKEN IN CREAMY MUSHROOM SAUCE

Ingredients
4 quarters of chicken
1 oz butter
1 tablespoonful vegetable oil
1 level tablespoonful onion (finely chopped)
$10\frac{1}{2}$ oz can condensed mushroom soup
$\frac{1}{4}$ pint milk
3 tablespoonsful single cream
1 teaspoonful fresh lemon juice

METHOD

Heat the butter and oil together in a pan with a well-fitting lid. Slowly fry the onion and chicken joints uncovered, until the joints begin to turn golden brown, turning them from time to time.

Combine the soup and milk together until smooth, then pour over the chicken. Cover the pan and simmer over a low heat for about 30 minutes, stirring from time to time.

When the joints are tender remove the lid, stir in the cream and lemon juice and serve with vegetables in season. (4 portions)

CHICKEN IN ORANGE AND ALMOND SAUCE

Ingredients

1 broiler chicken cut into serving pieces
½ teaspoonful salt
3 oz butter
1 oz plain flour
small pinch cinnamon
very small pinch ground ginger
¾ pint fresh orange juice (about 4 large oranges)
2 oz blanched almonds
2 oz seedless raisins
1 large orange (sliced)
enough cooked rice for 4 persons

METHOD

Wash the chicken well in cold water, then dry thoroughly. In a saucepan or large frying pan melt the butter, brown the chicken all over lightly and remove from the pan. Mix the flour, salt, cinnamon and ginger together; gradually blend with the butter to make a smooth paste. Add the orange juice a little at a time, to give a smooth sauce; cook, stirring all the time until the sauce bubbles and begins to thicken. Return the chicken to the pan together with the almonds and raisins, cover the pan with a lid, and cook at a simmering heat until the chicken is tender, approximately 45 minutes. Serve the chicken on a plate of hot rice, pour over the sauce and garnish with the slices of orange. (4 portions)

CHICKEN SALAD CAPRICE

Ingredients

1 large banana
1 large orange
8 oz cooked chicken
2 tablespoonsful lemon juice
3 tablespoonsful mayonnaise
2 tablespoonsful double cream
few black grapes for garnishing
crisp lettuce leaves

METHOD
Slice the banana into a bowl and turn over and over in the lemon juice.
Peel the orange, remove the pith and pips and add the segments to the
bowl. Cut the chicken into small pieces and add, also the mayonnaise
and cream. Mix all lightly together and set aside in a cool place for an
hour for the flavours to blend together.
TO SERVE Line a shallow bowl with the lettuce leaves, pile the chicken
salad in the centre and garnish with the halved and seeded grapes.

(3–4 portions)

CHICKEN WITH PINEAPPLE RICE

Ingredients

4 chicken portions

BATTER
4 oz plain flour
1 egg (size 4)
$\frac{1}{4}$ pint milk
salt and pepper to taste

RICE
8 oz hot cooked rice
**small can drained and chopped pineapple
pieces**
fat or oil for deep fat frying
2 tablespoonsful pineapple juice
**1 tablespoonful blanched and toasted almonds
(chopped)**

METHOD
Wash and thoroughly dry the chicken portions on a clean cloth. Once the fat or oil is hot enough for frying, dip each portion into the batter, drain off any excess batter and fry for about 20 minutes, or until they are tender, turning once or twice during cooking. Drain on absorbent paper when cooked and serve with the hot pineapple rice.

Cook the rice as for a curry, and leave in the saucepan, then add the pineapple pieces, juice and almonds, pile into a hot dish and serve.

(4 portions)

COUNTRY GRILLED CHICKEN

Ingredients
3–4 chicken quarters
4 rashers streaky bacon (diced)
4 oz mushrooms (sliced)
2 oz blanched almonds
1 level tablespoonful chopped chives
1 level tablespoonful chopped parsley
1½ oz butter
little melted butter

METHOD
Wipe the chicken with a clean damp cloth, then place in the base of the grill pan. Brush both sides with melted butter, and with the skin side down grill for 12–15 minutes. Turn the joints over and grill the other side until the joints are tender and golden brown.

In the meantime melt the 1½ oz of butter in a frying pan, add the bacon and almonds and lightly fry for a few minutes. Add the mushrooms and cook a further 5 minutes. Just before serving add the chives and parsley to the frying pan, stir for a minute then pour over the grilled chicken.

(3–4 portions)

DUCK AND ORANGE CASSEROLE

Ingredients
4–5 lb duck (jointed in 4 pieces)
seasoned flour for frying
fat for frying
2 onions
4 oz mushrooms
2 tomatoes (sliced)
2 oz raisins
grated rind and juice of 2 oranges
1 teaspoonful lemon juice
2 tablespoonsful port or brandy
$\frac{1}{2}$ pint stock
1 tablespoonful cornflour
salt and pepper
1 sliced orange

METHOD

Coat duck portions in the seasoned flour and fry in fat. Remove duck from the pan and keep warm. Slice onions and fry in the fat with mushrooms and tomatoes, then place in the bottom of an ovenproof casserole. Put the duck on top. Put raisins, orange rind, lemon juice, port and orange juice in the pan and heat, then add stock and bring to the boil. Thicken with the cornflour and add seasoning to taste. Pour over the duck, cover casserole and cook at approximately 350°F (180°C) or Mark 4 for about 1$\frac{1}{2}$ hours, or until the duck is tender.

Serve with cauliflower, peas and duchess potatoes. Garnish duck with the orange slices. No other sauces are necessary.   (4 portions)

DUCK WITH ORANGE SAUCE

Ingredients
1 Lincolnshire duckling (4$\frac{1}{2}$–5 lb dressed weight)
2 tablespoonsful cold water
3 oranges
watercress for garnishing

STUFFING
1 lb onions
2 oz fresh white breadcrumbs
2 teaspoonsful powdered sage
salt and pepper to taste

METHOD
TO MAKE THE STUFFING Peel and cut the onions into quarters and drop into a little boiling water. Parboil for 15 minutes, drain well then chop; add all other ingredients, and stuff the breast or body of the duckling.

Place a large piece of foil in the roasting pan, lay in the duckling and add the water. Wrap the foil loosely round the duckling and cook at approximately 375°F (190°C) or Mark 5 for about 2½ hours, when the leg joints should move easily.

Half an hour before the cooking time is finished, fold back the foil to brown the duckling, and add the juice from two of the oranges, baste once or twice during the remaining time.

Garnish with the orange slices cut from the remaining orange, which have been lightly fried in a little butter, and add sprigs of watercress just before serving. (4 portions) .

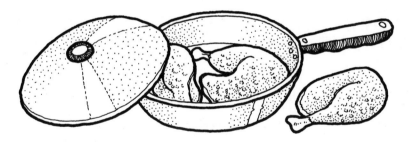

FRIED CHICKEN WITH PIQUANT SAUCE

Ingredients
4 quarters of chicken
2 oz plain flour
1 level teaspoonful dry mustard
1 level teaspoonful salt
freshly ground pepper
2 oz butter
2 oz bacon dripping

73

METHOD

Mix together the flour, mustard, salt and pepper. Coat the chicken joints
well in the seasoned flour. Using a frying pan with a lid, melt the butter
and dripping. Fry the chicken joints slowly until brown all over, then
cover the pan and cook very slowly for about 30 minutes, turning once
during cooking. When cooked serve with the Piquant Sauce. Plain boiled
rice goes very well with this dish.

SAUCE
1 oz butter
1 oz plain flour
1 level teaspoonful ready-made mustard
1 level teaspoonful Worcester sauce
¾ pint water
salt and pepper to taste

METHOD

In a small saucepan melt the butter, stir in the flour and cook, stirring
until brown, 2–3 minutes. Remove the pan from the heat and add
mustard, sauce and the water gradually, season and return the pan to the
heat. Cook stirring all the time until the sauce has thickened slightly.

Serve separately or poured over the chicken.   (4 portions)

GOSLING WITH SAGE, ONION AND WALNUT STUFFING

Ingredients

8 lb gosling
little flour (plain)
STUFFING
½ lb onions (peeled and chopped)
1 teaspoonful powdered sage
4 oz fresh white breadcrumbs
1½ oz finely chopped walnuts
1 egg
1½ oz melted butter
grated rind half lemon
2 teaspoonsful lemon juice
salt and pepper to taste
SAUCE
20 oz can gooseberries
½ oz butter

TO MAKE THE STUFFING Put the onions into a saucepan, cover with cold water, bring to the boil and simmer 5 minutes. Drain well in a sieve, pressing out any excess liquid. Mix the onions with the sage, bread-crumbs, walnuts and seasoning. Stir in the beaten egg, butter, lemon rind and juice, and place in the neck and/or body of the gosling.

Place a large piece of foil into the roasting pan, lay in the gosling and sprinkle the top with a little flour. Fold the foil loosely round the gosling and cook at approximately 375°F (190°C) or Mark 5 allowing 20 minutes to the pound. To test when done, place a small skewer into the leg joint, and if the liquid is pink give it a little longer in the oven. Half an hour before the cooking time is completed, fold back the foil to brown.

TO MAKE THE SAUCE Rub the gooseberries through a sieve, having first drained off the juice. Put the gooseberries into a small saucepan, add the butter and heat. Serve with the gosling and garnish with watercress.

(4–6 portions)

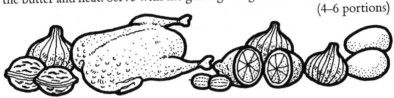

MOTHER'S JUGGED HARE

Ingredients
1 small hare (jointed)
approx. 2 oz dripping for frying
2–4 oz flour seasoned with salt and pepper
1 medium-sized onion
4 cloves
1 bouquet garni
1–2 wineglasses port wine
approx. 1 pint stock

METHOD

Wipe the joints with a clean damp cloth, and coat in seasoned flour. In a frying pan heat the dripping and fry the joints until they are well browned all over. Place the joints when fried into a deep casserole, add onion which has been peeled, cut in half and stuck with cloves, and bouquet garni. Put any remaining flour into the frying pan and cook until it browns, then slowly add the stock stirring until it thickens. Pour the stock into the casserole, and if required, add a little extra stock to cover the joints. Put on the lid and cook at approximately 300°F (150°C) or Mark 2 until tender, about 2–2½ hours.

Half an hour before serving, remove the onion and bouquet garni and add the port wine. Serve with redcurrant jelly. (4–6 portions)

PLAIN OR PARTY CHICKEN

Ingredients

2 chicken quarters
1½ oz butter
1 teaspoonful grated lemon rind
1 tablespoonful fresh lemon juice
¼ pint white wine or water
1 rounded dessertspoonful chopped parsley
salt and pepper to taste

PLAIN GARNISH
few sprigs watercress

PARTY GARNISH
2–4 slices pineapple
1 oz blanched and sliced almonds

METHOD
Either cut the chicken quarters in half or leave whole as desired. In a frying pan melt the butter and fry the chicken joints slowly on both sides until golden brown. Allow about 5 minutes on each side. Put the joints into an ovenproof casserole, add rind, juice, wine or water, parsley and salt and pepper. Cover with a lid and cook at approximately 350°F (180°C) or Mark 4 for about 45 minutes or until the joints are tender.
TO SERVE Place the joints on a hot serving dish, and keep hot while thickening the casserole juices. Garnish with watercress.
TO SERVE FOR A PARTY Just before the joints are cooked brown the almonds in a little butter, brush the pineapple with butter and heat through. Serve pineapple rings round the joints, almonds sprinkled over the top and the casserole juices poured over the joints. Garnish with parsley. (2–4 portions)

76

QUICK CHICKEN AND HAM PIE

Ingredients

8 oz cooked diced chicken
4 oz cooked diced ham
10½ oz can condensed chicken soup
¼ pint single cream
1 small packet frozen peas (cooked)
1 small packet potato crisps

METHOD

Put the soup into a saucepan, stir in the cream and heat very gently. Add the chicken, ham and peas and continue stirring until thoroughly heated through. Pour the ingredients into a hot serving dish, and sprinkle the crisps over the surface. Serve at once. (4 portions)

ROAST CHICKEN WITH ONION STUFFING

Ingredients

1 tomato
2 oz mushrooms
2 salad onions
2 oz soft breadcrumbs
1 teaspoonful paprika
salt and pepper
egg to bind
1 roasting chicken

METHOD

Skin the tomato and chop with the mushrooms and onion until fine. Mix all well together, add breadcrumbs, paprika, salt and pepper and bind with a little egg. Push it into the neck of the chicken, place it in the roasting-pan, cover with a piece of bacon and roast in the usual way at approximately 400°F (200°C) or Mark 6, allowing 20 minutes to the pound. Serve with gravy from the roasting-pan.   (3–4 portions)

SAVOURY STUFFED CHICKEN

Ingredients
**3 lb chicken
1 oz butter
3 oz onion (finely chopped)
3 oz celery (finely chopped)
6 oz pork sausage meat
½ level teaspoonful grated lemon rind
salt, pepper and nutmeg to taste**

METHOD
Remove the giblets, wash and place in a small saucepan, cover with water and simmer until tender. Strain before serving as gravy.

In a small frying pan melt the butter, add the onion and celery and cook gently over a low heat until they are soft and golden. Stir in the remaining ingredients, being very careful with the seasoning if sausage meat is used.

When thoroughly mixed, put the stuffing loosely into the neck of the chicken. Place the chicken in the roasting pan, cover the breast with 2 or 3 slices of fat bacon and roast allowing 20 minutes to the pound and 20 minutes over at approximately 375°F (190°C) or Mark 5.

If the chicken is roasted in a covered pan remove the lid at least 20 minutes before cooking is finished to brown the bird.   (4 portions)

STRAWBERRY CHICKEN

Ingredients
**4 chicken legs (boned)
2 oz butter
small punnet strawberries
4 tablespoonsful double cream
salt and pepper
few chives (chopped)**

METHOD
Flatten the chicken legs and fry gently in the melted butter. Season well, remove from the pan and keep hot.

Halve the strawberries and fry gently in the pan until just cooked. Place on the chicken.

Add the cream to the juices in the pan, stir well and allow to heat, but DO NOT BOIL.

Pour juices over the chicken and serve sprinkled with chopped chives.

(4 portions)

TURKEY WITH CORN AND CHESTNUT STUFFING

Ingredients
12–14 lb turkey
few slices of fat bacon

STUFFING
12 oz can chestnut purée
11 oz can giant corn niblets
6 oz fresh white breadcrumbs
4 oz dripping
1 lb sausage meat
1 tablespoonful chopped parsley
salt and pepper to taste

METHOD
TO MAKE THE STUFFING In a basin break the chestnut purée down with a fork, add the drained corn, breadcrumbs, sausage meat, parsley and seasoning, finally binding all together with the melted dripping. Stuff the neck and body of the turkey.

Place a large piece of foil in the roasting pan, put in the bird, add the bacon to the breast and fold the foil loosely round the bird. Cook at approximately 325°F (160°C) or Mark 3 for about 4½–5 hours. Half an hour before the cooking time is finished, remove the bacon, fold back the foil to brown the bird. (20 portions)

FISH

I've always had a fondness for fish and it's so tasty, easily digestable, full of flavour and quick to prepare and cook. Although there is a wide variety to choose from, always buy them fresh when they are in season.

Most of these recipes are specific in the type of fish used, but with a little imagination and a look in the larder, you'll see how easily they can be adapted by using other fish. For instance, in the recipes for Creamed Haddock, Fish and Cheese Crumble or Fish Curry almost any other white or smoked fish could be used to suit your palate or your pocket. It also helps to ring the changes in the family's diet.

Finally, for all those special occasions, why not try Creamed Scampi, Trout with Almond Sauce or Dressed Crab.

APPLE STUFFED HERRINGS

Ingredients

4 large herrings (boned)
salt and pepper
½ lb eating apples
3 oz fresh white breadcrumbs
1 small onion (finely chopped)
1 level dessertspoonful granulated sugar
1 oz melted butter

METHOD

Season the herrings with the salt and pepper. Peel, core and chop the apples and mix this together with the onion, two-thirds of the breadcrumbs and sugar.

Divide this mixture into four and put one portion between the fillets of each herring. Place the stuffed herrings into a greased ovenproof dish, sprinkle on the remaining breadcrumbs and trickle over the melted butter. Bake at approximately 350°F (180°C) or Mark 4 for about 25 minutes or until they're cooked and golden brown.

Serve with either a tossed green salad and brown bread and butter or mashed potatoes and a green vegetable. (4 portions)

CREAMED HADDOCK

Ingredients
1 oz margarine
1 oz plain flour
¾ pint milk
3 oz grated Cheddar cheese
1 lb smoked haddock (cooked and flaked)
2 hard-boiled eggs (chopped)
pepper to taste

METHOD
In a saucepan melt the margarine, stir in the flour and cook for 2–3 minutes. Remove the pan from the heat and gradually add the milk, beating well all the time. When all the milk has been added bring the sauce to the boil, stirring all the time and cook until it thickens. Stir in the fish, cheese and eggs in this order. Re-heat until almost boiling, pour into a hot ovenproof dish, sprinkle on the remaining cheese and brown under the grill. Serve very hot.   (4–5 portions)

CREAMED SCAMPI

Ingredients
1 oz butter
½ lb scampi
little plain flour
½ pint double cream
salt, pepper and paprika pepper
little lemon juice
chopped parsley for garnish
3 lemon wedges

METHOD
Melt the butter in a frying pan or shallow fireproof dish. Toss the drained scampi in the flour to coat all over. Fry very gently over a low heat, shaking the pan from time to time. Be careful not to overcook the scampi.

When the scampi are cooked, add the cream and cook for a minute or two again over a low heat. Season with salt, pepper and lemon juice, then add a pinch of paprika to give a little colour. Serve in the dish or turn out into a hot serving dish, and sprinkle with chopped parsley. (3 portions)

CRUNCHY TAIL OF HADDOCK

Ingredients
1–1½ lb filleted haddock tail
2 oz butter
1 teaspoonful salt or to taste
pepper
cornflake crumbs
mayonnaise

METHOD

Melt the butter in the grill pan, brush the fish on the skin side and grill for 3 minutes. Turn the fish over carefully and brush with butter, then continue grilling for a further 9 minutes, basting two or three times with butter. Spread or brush the fish with a thin layer of mayonnaise, add a little more seasoning and then sprinkle on the crumbs to make a layer. Baste again with the butter and grill a further one to two minutes until the crumbs are golden brown and crisp. Serve at once.   (3–4 portions)

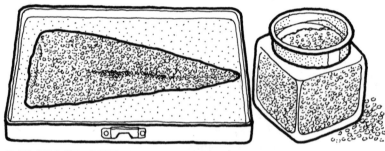

DEVILLED HERRING ROES

Ingredients
2 oz butter
4 herring roes (cooked)
made mustard to taste
salt and pepper
1 teaspoonful Worcester sauce
4 slices of toast
4 anchovies

METHOD

Melt the butter and cream the roes with it. Add the made mustard, seasoning and sauce. Spread this mixture on the toast, put on the anchovies and heat under the grill for only a few minutes. Serve at once. (4 portions)

DRESSED CRAB

Ingredients
    1 crab
salt and pepper
lemon juice or vinegar
white breadcrumbs
1 chopped hard-boiled egg
little finely chopped parsley
salad in season

METHOD
After the crab has been cleaned by the fishmonger, remove the claws, legs and body. Put all the brown meat in one basin and all the white meat in another. Mash the brown meat with salt, pepper and lemon juice, add sufficient breadcrumbs to stiffen the texture slightly and pile into each end of the shell. Flake the white meat and put this in the centre. Garnish with egg and parsley and serve with salad.

FISH AND CHEESE CRUMBLE

Ingredients
    1 lb cod fillet
$\frac{1}{4}$ pint milk
1 egg yolk (beaten)
salt and pepper
1 level dessertspoonful chopped parsley
2 large tomatoes (skinned and sliced)
approx. $\frac{1}{2}$ oz butter
CRUMBLE
1 oz butter or lard
4 oz self-raising flour
2 oz grated Cheddar cheese
small pinch cayenne pepper

METHOD
Wash the fish and cut if necessary to fit into a frying pan which has a lid, or alternatively an ovenproof dish with a lid. Pour on the milk and simmer until cooked about 10 minutes. Remove the cod onto a dish and flake. Pour the liquid the fish was cooked in into a small jug or basin. Add the beaten egg yolk to the milk, season with salt and pepper, add the parsley and stir well together.

Grease a 1½ pint ovenproof casserole, put the fish in and pour over the liquid. Arrange the sliced tomatoes on top.

To make the crumble: Rub the 1 oz of butter or lard into the sieved flour until it resembles fine breadcrumbs, stir in the cheese, salt and cayenne pepper. Sprinkle the crumble on top of the tomatoes and spread evenly. Use the remaining butter to flake over the crumble. Bake at approximately 350°F (180°C) or Mark 4 for about 35 minutes, then raise the temperature slightly to brown the top for about a further 10 minutes. Garnish with a sprig of parsley and serve.   (4 portions)

FISH CURRY

Ingredients   **1 lb filleted cod or similar fish**
1½ oz butter or butter fat (ghee)
2 medium-sized tomatoes
1 medium-sized onion
2 dessertspoonsful powdered dhania or fresh parsley
1 teaspoonful garam-masala
1 teaspoonful turmeric
1½ teaspoonsful salt
½ teaspoonful chilli powder
1 dessertspoonful desiccated coconut
2 small cloves of garlic
1 tablespoonful fresh lemon juice

METHOD
Into a saucepan put the finely chopped onion, garlic and dhania or parsley and gently fry in the butter or ghee. Next add the turmeric, garam-masala, salt, chilli powder and coconut, mix well and allow to cook for a few minutes. Add the sliced tomatoes and fry until tender; stir in the lemon juice and mix all well together. Cook this mixture gently for 4–5 minutes, then add the well-washed and drained fish which has been cut into pieces, but not too small, and leaving the skin on. Cover the fish very carefully with the sauce, and when it starts to boil cover with a lid and allow the curry to simmer for 7–10 minutes, just until the fish is cooked. Do not let it become soft and mushy. If you prefer a drier curry, remove the lid while it is simmering. Serve with a dish of long grain rice.

(4 portions)

GRILLED PLAICE WITH SOUR CREAM SAUCE

Ingredients
4 fillets of plaice with bone
1 oz butter
½ pint fish stock from bones
¼ pint sour cream
2 sweet pickled cucumbers
salt and pepper

METHOD
Cover the fish bones with water and cook gently to give a fish stock. Slice the pickled cucumbers finely and wash the fish.

Put the fish into a greased ovenproof dish, dot with the butter, season with salt and pepper and grill under a moderate heat for about 5–6 minutes or until tender.

Remove the fish to a heated serving dish or leave in the dish in which it was cooked and keep hot.

Pour off half a pint of the fish stock and put into a clean saucepan, add the sour cream and bring to the boil. Add the finely sliced cucumbers and continue cooking for a further minute. Pour the sauce over the fish and serve at once. (4 portions)

KIPPER AND EGG CROQUETTES

Ingredients
8 oz kipper fillets (minced)
2 hard-boiled eggs (finely chopped)
1 oz butter
1 oz plain flour
¼ pint milk
1 teaspoonful parsley (chopped)
pepper and salt to taste

TO COAT
little well-beaten egg
quantity of lightly browned breadcrumbs
fat or oil for frying

METHOD
Make the sauce by heating the fat and flour together in a saucepan. Stir until the flour is cooked and then remove the saucepan from the heat and

gradually add the milk, stirring all the time to keep the sauce smooth. When all the milk has been added, stir in the seasoning, parsley, eggs, fillets and return the saucepan to the heat. Allow the mixture to come to the boil and then turn the mixture out onto a plate or dish to become quite cold.

When the mixture is cold divide into 7 or 8 equal portions, and with a little flour on the hands mould into rounds, rolls or any shape desired. Brush them with the well-beaten egg and toss in breadcrumbs.

Fry in shallow or deep fat as desired until thoroughly heated through and golden brown, approximately 3–4 minutes.

Drain on absorbent paper and serve immediately.　　　　(7–8 portions)

KIPPER PIZZA

Ingredients　　　　　$\frac{1}{4}$ **oz fresh yeast**
1 level teaspoonful caster sugar
2 tablespoonsful of warm water
1 egg
4 oz plain flour
$\frac{1}{2}$ level teaspoonful salt

METHOD

Sieve the flour and salt into a warmed bowl, and keep in a warm place. Cream the yeast and sugar together, add the beaten egg and the warmed water. Make a well in the centre of the flour and pour in the liquid. Beat the mixture thoroughly with a wooden spoon or by hand, until all the ingredients are evenly blended.

Cover the basin with a clean cloth and leave in a warm place to rise to double its size about 45 minutes.

Turn the dough out onto a lightly floured board and knead for about 1 minute. Place the dough on a lightly floured baking tin and press into a round 8–9 in. in diameter, building up the edges until they are about $\frac{3}{4}$–1 in. high. Leave to prove for 10 minutes.

Fill the centre with the selected filling, and bake at approximately 400°F (200°C) or Mark 6 for 15–20 minutes.

N.B. ALTERNATIVE BASES FOR THE FILLING
4 oz of plain scone mixture OR
4 oz of short crust pastry, which is made into a flan

Ingredients	**CHEESE FILLING**
	4 oz kipper fillets
	1 egg
	⅓ pint milk
	1 tablespoonful white breadcrumbs
	2 oz (roughly grated) Parmesan cheese
	a scrape of nutmeg
	very small pinch cayenne pepper
	pinch of salt

METHOD

Cut half of the kipper fillets into small pieces, and the other half into thin strips, cutting each fillet lengthwise.

Mix the small pieces of kipper, cheese and all seasoning together and spoon into the base. Beat the egg into the milk and when well beaten add the breadcrumbs and mix well.

Pour this mixture over the ingredients in the base and decorate with the thin strips of kipper fillet.

Ingredients	**TOMATO FILLING**
	1 small can tomato soup
	¼ pint milk
	large pinch of mixed herbs
	4 oz kipper fillets

METHOD

Empty the tin of soup into a saucepan, add the milk and bring to the boil. Allow this mixture to cool before adding the herbs and half of the kipper fillets, which have been cut into small pieces.

Cut the remainder of the kipper fillets into thin strips lengthwise. Pour the mixture into the base and decorate with the thin strips of kipper fillets in a criss-cross pattern.

MARINADED DABS

Ingredients

2 English dabs (skinned and filleted)
6 tablespoonsful olive or vegetable oil
3 tablespoonsful lemon juice
1 small onion (finely chopped)
small pinch rosemary

METHOD

Place the dabs in a dish, then add the onion and rosemary. Mix together the oil and lemon juice and pour over the other ingredients. Marinade the dabs in this mixture for about 2 hours, turning them occasionally.

To cook, drain the dabs from the marinade, and either grill till golden brown, basting them with the juice from time to time or coat in beaten egg and breadcrumbs, and grill or fry until golden brown. Serve garnished with lemon slices and parsley.   (4 portions)

PRAWN SALAD WITH HOT MAYONNAISE

Ingredients

SALAD
6 oz prawns (fresh, canned or frozen)
1 lettuce
few spring onions
½ cucumber
2 tomatoes
2 hard-boiled eggs

MAYONNAISE
2 eggs
2 tablespoonsful double cream
1 tablespoonful French mustard
1 tablespoonful olive oil
3 dessertspoonsful white vinegar
3 level teaspoonsful caster sugar
salt and pepper to taste

METHOD

Shred the lettuce, slice the cucumber and eggs, cut the tomatoes into wedges. Put the lettuce in the centre of a serving dish. Arrange the cucumber and hard-boiled eggs alternately round the edge of the dish.

Put the prawns onto the lettuce and surround with the tomatoes and onions.

TO MAKE THE MAYONNAISE Beat the eggs and stir in all other ingredients. Put the basin over a pan of boiling water, and cook, stirring all the time until the mayonnaise is thick and creamy. Serve at once with the chilled prawn salad. (4 portions)

PRAWNS WITH MACARONI

Ingredients
6 oz macaroni
2 oz grated Cheddar cheese
2 oz fresh prawns
1 can condensed tomato soup
$\frac{1}{2}$ oz butter
$\frac{1}{4}$ pint milk
seasoning to taste

METHOD
Cook the macaroni as directed on the packet, drain well and keep hot. In the meantime heat the soup in a saucepan, add the milk, butter, seasoning, prawns and cheese. Once the ingredients are hot add the cooked macaroni and stir until evenly blended. Pour into a heatproof dish and serve immediately.

N.B. An alternative way of serving this dish is to arrange the cooked macaroni round the edge of a heatproof dish and pour the other ingredients into the centre. (2–3 portions)

SAUCY FISH PIE

Ingredients

12 oz short crust pastry
milk to glaze

FILLING
1 oz soft margarine
1 oz plain flour
$\frac{1}{2}$ pint milk
salt and pepper
4 oz prawns (peeled)
2 oz cucumber (diced)
2 hard-boiled eggs (chopped)
2 oz Cheddar cheese (grated)
$\frac{1}{2}$ stuffed olive
cucumber twist and parsley

METHOD

TO MAKE THE FILLING Put margarine, flour, milk and seasoning into a saucepan over a medium heat. Stir continuously, bring to the boil and cook 1–2 minutes until thickened and smooth. Stir in prawns, cucumber, eggs and cheese. Set aside to cool.

Divide pastry into two. Roll each piece out on a lightly floured board to an oval about 8 in. long. (Use a pie dish as a guide.) Cut each oval into a fish shape.

Place one piece on a baking tin, damp the edge with water and fill, leaving about $\frac{1}{4}$ in. free round the edge.

Place second oval on top, press edges well together and flute. Mark top with a criss-cross pattern and make a hole for the eye.

Brush with milk and bake at approximately 400°F (200°C) or Mark 6 for about 25–30 minutes.

Place olive in hole for the eye and cucumber twist to represent the fin. Garnish with parsley and serve at once. (4 portions)

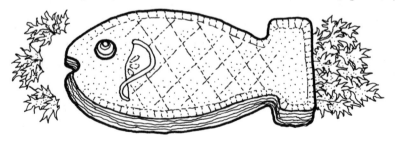

SAUCY FRIED HERRINGS

Ingredients   **4 large herrings (scaled and cleaned)**
1 oz butter
seasoned flour

SAUCE
1 oz butter
2 medium onions (finely chopped)
2 medium cooking apples
1–2 level teaspoonsful curry powder
1 level tablespoonful redcurrant jelly
salt and pepper
carton yogurt (plain)
parsley (chopped)

METHOD
Wash and dry the herrings, then roll in seasoned flour. Lightly fry in
butter for 3–4 minutes on each side until crisp, tender and golden brown.
   Keep herrings hot while making sauce.

TO MAKE THE SAUCE Fry onions in butter until transparent and
golden brown. Peel, core and coarsely chop apples, add to onions, cook
for a few minutes until almost tender, then add jelly and curry powder.
When all blended well together, season well.
   Remove pan from the heat and pour in yogurt, mix well. Return pan to
heat and re-heat very gently, but do not boil.
   To serve. Pour the sauce over the herrings and sprinkle with parsley.

(4 portions)

SMOKED COD

Ingredients   **1 oz butter**
1 oz plain flour
¾ pint milk
1 lb smoked cod (cooked)
3 oz Cheddar cheese (grated)
2 hard-boiled eggs (chopped)
salt and pepper

METHOD

Melt the butter in a saucepan, stir in the flour and cook for 2–3 minutes. Take the pan from the stove and add the milk gradually, beating all the time. Return the pan to the stove and bring the sauce to the boil, stirring all the time. Cook until it has thickened.

Flake the fish and stir into the sauce, then add the cheese, seasonings and, finally, the hard-boiled egg. Heat again until ALMOST BOILING POINT, then pour into a heated ovenproof dish, sprinkle some grated cheese over the top and brown under a hot grill. (4 portions)

SOLE IN WINE

Ingredients

2 small onions
$\frac{1}{4}$ lb 'cap' mushrooms
4 soles (filleted)
$\frac{1}{2}$ pint red wine
seasonings
$\frac{1}{4}$ lb shrimps
sliced lemon

METHOD

Slice the onions, chop the mushrooms and fry them lightly. Put the sole fillets in an ovenproof dish with the onions and mushrooms on top. Add the wine and seasoning and cook in the oven until the fish is tender. Heat the shrimps and serve them as a garnish with slices of lemon.

You can use white wine if preferred, but the dish will lack colour.

(4 portions)

STUFFED COD CUTLETS

Ingredients

4 cod cutlets
salt and pepper
juice of $\frac{1}{2}$ a lemon
1 small onion (chopped)
$\frac{1}{2}$ oz butter
1 oz fresh white breadcrumbs
$\frac{1}{4}$ teaspoonful tarragon or thyme
1 dessertspoonful milk
$\frac{1}{2}$ pint prawn, cheese or parsley sauce

METHOD

Place the cutlets into a greased ovenproof dish, having first removed the centre bone with a sharp knife. Season with salt and pepper and sprinkle with a few drops of lemon juice. In a small frying pan melt the butter and cook the onion until soft and transparent, then add the breadcrumbs, tarragon or thyme, milk, salt and pepper and remaining lemon juice. Form the mixture into four portions and place in the centre of each cutlet. Cover the dish with a lid and bake at approximately 375°F (190°C) or Mark 5 for about 20 minutes.

During the latter part of the cooking time make up the sauce, and serve poured over the fish or separately in a sauce boat. (4 portions)

TROUT WITH ALMOND SAUCE

Ingredients

3 fresh trout
2 oz plain flour ⎱ **seasoned flour**
salt and pepper ⎰
2 oz butter
1 dessertspoonful vegetable oil

SAUCE
2 oz butter
1½–2 oz sliced or split almonds
juice of 1 lemon
little black pepper

METHOD

Clean, wash and drain the fish. Coat all over in the seasoned flour. In a large frying pan heat the butter and oil together, and when hot, put the fish in one at a time. Cook approximately 5 minutes, then carefully turn the fish over, taking care not to pierce the flesh. Continue cooking for about another 5 minutes. Lift the fish out, put onto a warm serving dish and keep hot.

Wipe out the frying pan with absorbent paper, then heat the remaining 2 oz butter, add the almonds and cook until golden brown about 2–3 minutes. Add the lemon juice and black pepper, mix all together, then pour over the trout and serve at once. (3 portions)

VEGETABLES

I decided not to include the boiling and steaming of everyday vegetables in this section as we all have our own particular ways of doing this to suit individual tastes. On the other hand I get fed up with people saying we British are unimaginative in the way we cook and serve vegetables.

So here are just a few simple ideas, nothing elaborate, to show them we can and are prepared to do something a little different with the wide variety of excellent fresh vegetables we have available in this country.

As you will see a number of them are braised in the oven and are suitable for serving with the roast meat of your choice.

ARTICHOKES AND VINAIGRETTE DRESSING

Ingredients   **VINAIGRETTE DRESSING**
4 tablespoonsful best quality salad oil
2 tablespoonsful white wine vinegar
1 teaspoonful finely chopped shallots
salt and pepper to taste

METHOD
Mix the oil, vinegar and shallots well together until evenly blended then add seasoning to taste.

Artichokes: Cut the stalks off closely, boil in salted water until a leaf pulls out easily. When cooked drain well. Serve hot or cold with vinaigrette dressing.

Eat by pulling out the leaves with the fingers; eating only the fleshy base, discard the fibrous interior, and then enjoy the creamy heart.

An original and simple hors d'oeuvre.

ASPARAGUS WITH MINT

Ingredients   **1 bundle Evesham asparagus**
1 sprig mint
salted boiling water
melted butter

METHOD

Scrape the butt ends of the asparagus. Tie in one portion bundles with thin string or cotton. Put the bundles into a large pan of boiling salted water, add the mint, cover with a lid and cook for about 15–20 minutes, depending on the size of the sticks. Drain on a clean cloth, untie the bundles and serve with lots of melted butter. (3 portions)

BROAD BEANS AND MUSHROOMS

Ingredients

1 small onion (chopped)
2 lb broad beans
¾ pint brown stock
little thyme
1 bay leaf
¼ lb mushrooms (sliced)
1 oz butter
1 oz plain flour
1 teaspoonful parsley (chopped)
1 tablespoonful lemon juice
salt and pepper

METHOD

Cook the onions and beans in boiling stock with thyme, bay leaf and a little salt for 15–20 minutes. Fry the mushrooms in butter until tender. Add them to the cooked beans. Add the flour to the remaining butter in the pan and cook until golden brown. Blend in the stock from the beans, stir this into the beans and mushrooms. Take out thyme and bay leaf. Stir over a gentle heat until just boiling. Add the parsley, lemon juice and seasoning, and serve hot. (4 portions)

CHEESY CUCUMBERS

Ingredients

4 small thin cucumbers
2 egg yolks
¼ pint single cream
½ teaspoonful vinegar
4 tablespoonsful Lancashire cheese (crumbled)
chopped parsley

METHOD

Peel the cucumbers and cut into conveniently sized lengths. Simmer in salted water for 10 minutes and drain. Place them in a greased, shallow ovenproof dish. Beat the eggs and cream together, then cook over a low heat, stirring until the mixture is thick, then add the vinegar. Pour the sauce over the cucumbers, sprinkle the top with the cheese and parsley and bake for 15 minutes in a moderate oven at approximately 375°F (190°C) or Mark 5. Serve at once. (3–4 portions)

CORN FRITTERS

Ingredients
3 egg yolks
salt and pepper
1 breakfast cup corn
1 oz plain flour
3 egg whites
deep fat for frying

METHOD

Cream the egg yolks lightly in a basin, stir in the seasoning, corn and flour. Whisk the egg whites until they are stiff and fold into the mixture. Drop tablespoonsful of the mixture into hot fat and fry until golden brown all over. Drain and serve at once. (2 portions)

DANISH PICKLED BEETROOTS

Ingredients
1 lb beetroots
½ pint malt vinegar
¼ pint water
2 oz sugar

METHOD

Wash the beetroots but do not peel, cook them slowly in water until they are tender, about 1½–2 hours. Allow to cool, then peel and slice them. Put them into hot jars, while bringing the vinegar, water and sugar to the boil. Once it has boiled, pour over the beetroot until it is completely covered.

These pickled beetroots will keep for 2–3 weeks, or longer if strips of raw horseradish are boiled with the vinegar.

Serve with any kind of cold meat and salad.

DAWN POTATOES

Ingredients
$\frac{1}{4}$ **lb mashed potatoes**
1 oz butter
1 medium-sized carrot (grated)
1 egg
2 tablespoonsful milk
salt and pepper
little finely chopped parsley

METHOD

In a basin beat $\frac{1}{2}$ oz of butter and the grated carrot into the hot mashed potato.

Mix the egg, milk and seasoning together.

Heat the remaining butter in a small saucepan, add the egg mixture and stir over a medium heat until set.

Serve the potato mixture in a ring on a hot plate and pile the egg into the centre. Sprinkle with the parsley just before serving.　　　(1 portion)

EGG AND VEGETABLE SCRAMBLE

Ingredients
2 oz butter
3 oz mushrooms (quartered)
3 tomatoes (peeled and quartered)
$\frac{1}{4}$ **lb cooked peas**
5–6 oz cooked diced potatoes
4 eggs
salt and pepper to taste
little grated cheese (optional)

METHOD

Melt the butter in a frying pan, add the potatoes and mushrooms and cook 1–2 minutes, then add the tomatoes and peas. When they are thoroughly heated through add 4 lightly beaten eggs, pouring them all over the vegetables, and season to taste. Finally add a little grated cheese and cook slowly with a lid or plate over the top until the eggs are set, about 10 minutes. Serve hot from the pan or on a hot serving dish.

(4 portions)

EMETT BAKED POTATO SPECIAL

Ingredients   **3 large or medium sized potatoes**
                               3 rashers of back bacon
                               1 medium sized onion
                               salt and pepper
                               1 tablespoonful grated cheese (Parmesan type)

METHOD

Scrub the potatoes well, dry, prick with a fork and rub the skins with a little butter.

Bake at approximately 425°F (220°C) or Mark 7 until soft, about 1–1½ hours according to size.

   When cooked cut off the top, scoop out the pulp and mix with the cooked bacon and onion, season and refill the potato shells.

   Sprinkle with grated cheese and brown in the oven or under the grill.

(3 portions)

GAZPACHO

(to make this, a food-mixer with a liquidiser is required)
Ingredients   **1 lemon (cut into quarters)**
                               2 green peppers
                               1 cucumber
                               2 lb fresh tomatoes (cut in halves)
                               1 onion (cut in quarters)
                               pinch garlic salt
                               2 tablespoonsful vinegar
                               2 tablespoonsful olive oil
                               seasoning to taste

METHOD

Remove the pips from the lemon, remove the seeds from the peppers and cut into pieces. Cut three-quarters of the cucumber into thick slices. Add all the ingredients in batches into the liquidiser, and bring them down to a pulp, then season to your own taste. Pour into individual glasses and put into the refrigerator. Serve with a topping of diced cucumber (using the remaining cucumber), tiny croutons of toast and a little chopped onion.

(6–8 portions)

GLAZED CARROTS

Ingredients

1½ lb carrots
1 oz butter
1 teaspoonful sugar
small quantity of stock

METHOD

Scrape and wash the carrots, then cut into thin slices, put them into an ovenproof dish, add the sugar, butter and enough stock to cover them. Put on lid and bake 375°F (190°C) or mark 5 about ½ hour. By the time the carrots are cooked the liquid will have evaporated and the carrots will be coated with a thick glaze.   (4 portions)

MUSHROOM PUDDING

Ingredients

½ lb suet crust pastry
¾ lb mushrooms
½ lb streaky bacon (green bacon for preference)
pinch thyme
salt and pepper
1 oz butter
¼ pint stock or water

METHOD

Line a 2-pint basin with the pastry, keeping aside sufficient to cover the top of the basin. Trim and cut the bacon into strips, cook in the heated butter until light golden brown in colour. Prepare and slice the mushrooms, then put a layer into the basin, then a layer of bacon and season. Continue with alternating layers and seasoning, and pack the basin tightly. Add the stock or water and the butter left in the pan, cover with the remaining pastry, having dampened the edges with a little water, and seal. Cover with a piece of greased greaseproof paper, leaving room for the pudding to rise; tie a pudding cloth firmly over this, and then boil in a covered pan for approx. 2 hours.   (4–6 portions)

POTATO BACON TOPPERS

Ingredients

10 middle-cut rashers
4 large potatoes
small knob of butter
1 tablespoonful milk
pepper
1 oz cheese (grated)
sprig of parsley

METHOD

Scrub the potatoes and score with a knife round the sides. Bake in the oven until they are cooked through, about 1½ hours at approximately 425°F (220°C) or Mark 7.

Cut the rind from all the bacon and reserve 8 rashers for garnishing later. Grill or fry the remaining bacon and cut or chop into small pieces. Just before the potatoes are cooked put the butter and milk to heat in a basin. As soon as the potatoes are cooked, cut in half, and scoop out the inside into the basin with the milk and butter. Beat all well together, and season with the pepper and add the chopped bacon. When mixed pile back into the potato skins, sprinkle with grated cheese and either put back into the oven or under the grill for the cheese to melt. Fry the 8 remaining rashers and garnish the potatoes with them, also a small sprig of parsley.

(4 portions)

RING-A-DING TOMMY

Ingredients

1 lb home-grown tomatoes (chopped)
4 chives (chopped)
1 pint chicken stock
½ oz powdered gelatine
1 tablespoonful salad cream
2 tablespoonsful dairy cream
4 oz cheese (finely grated)
4 oz ham (finely chopped)
4 chives (chopped)
salt and pepper
little chopped parsley

Cook tomatoes and four chives in the stock until they form a pulp. Dissolve the gelatine in 2 tablespoonsful of water, and put over hot water until dissolved thoroughly. Stir in the tomato mixture. Pour into a ring mould and leave to set.

Mix together the salad cream, cream, cheese, ham, parsley, chives and seasoning. Turn out the mould when set and fill the centre with the cheese mixture.

Serve garnished with watercress. (4 portions)

SAVOURY CARROT BAKE

Ingredients

$\frac{3}{4}$ **lb carrots**
white sauce (1 oz butter, 1 oz plain flour,
 $\frac{1}{4}$ pint milk and $\frac{1}{4}$ pint carrot liquor)
4 oz Cheddar cheese (grated)
$\frac{3}{4}$ lb potatoes (mashed)
little chopped parsley (for garnish)

METHOD

Peel and slice the carrots and boil until tender. Make a white sauce with the butter, flour, milk and carrot liquor, season and add 2 oz cheese. Drain the carrots, put them into an ovenproof dish, and cover with the sauce. Add the remainder of the cheese to the mashed potato and season. Spread the potato over the carrot mixture, or pipe if preferred, and brush with a little milk. Bake at approximately 400°F (200°C) or Mark 6 for about 30 minutes. Garnish with chopped parsley.

Eat this dish on its own or serve it with an escalop of veal fried in egg and breadcrumbs. (4 portions)

STUFFED MARROW

Ingredients   **1 medium-sized marrow (cut in half
                         lengthwise)**
                     ½ lb cooked minced bacon or meat
                     2 large carrots (cooked and diced)
                     1 large onion (chopped and fried)
                     1 hard-boiled egg (chopped)
                     1 level tablespoonful sultanas
                     1 level tablespoonful chopped nuts
                     salt and pepper
                     little tomato sauce
                     little finely grated cheese

METHOD

Scoop out the seeds from the marrow, and cook in water until almost
tender. Drain well then put into an ovenproof dish.

In a basin mix together the bacon or meat, carrots, onion, egg, sultanas,
nuts and season to taste. Bind these all together with the tomato sauce,
and when evenly blended fill the hollowed out marrow.

Sprinkle the top with the grated cheese and bake at approximately
400°F (200°C) or Mark 6 for about ½ an hour. Serve piping hot with new
potatoes.   (4–6 portions)

STUFFED ONIONS

Ingredients   **4 large onions**
                     ¼ pint white sauce
                     1 tablespoonful tomato chutney
                     2 oz cooked minced meat
                     1 oz breadcrumbs

METHOD

Boil the onions in boiling salted water until they are tender but still have
some crispness to them. In the meantime, make the sauce, using the onion
liquor. Add the tomato chutney. Heat the meat and breadcrumbs together and mix with a little of the sauce. When the onions are ready,
scoop out the centres, chop them and add to the meat mixture. Spoon
this mixture into the onions and serve on a hot dish. Put any excess filling
round the onions, then pour over the remaining sauce.   (4 portions)

SWEET 'N' SOUR LETTUCE

Ingredients
**1 crisp lettuce
1 finely chopped onion
½ lb finely grated carrot
2 hard–boiled eggs**

**DRESSING
¼ pint real double dairy cream
⅛ pint (2½ fl. oz) wine vinegar
2 level tablespoonsful caster sugar
salt and pepper to taste**

METHOD
Beat the cream, sugar and seasonings together and let them stand for about 5 minutes. Then gradually add the vinegar. Shred the lettuce finely and toss in the dressing. Arrange all the salad ingredients in a bowl and top with sliced hard-boiled eggs. (3–4 portions)

TOMATO RASCALS

Ingredients
**8 large home-grown tomatoes
2 oz powdered gelatine
1 pint stock
½ cooked onion (finely chopped)
6 oz cooked pork (finely chopped)
little parsley
seasoning to taste**

METHOD
Dissolve the gelatine in the stock in a basin over hot water. Cut the tomatoes in half, scoop out the pulp and sieve into the stock. Add the onion, finely chopped parsley and season to taste.

Leave the mixture to cool and then spoon carefully into the tomato shells. Leave to set and serve chilled. (4 portions)

VEGETABLE CASSEROLE

Ingredients
$\frac{1}{2}$ cauliflower
$\frac{1}{2}$ lb raw new carrots
1 lettuce
1 lb new potatoes
$\frac{1}{2}$ lb peas
few sprigs mint
salt and pepper
2 oz dairy butter

METHOD

Break the cauliflower into small pieces, cut the carrots into thin strips and pull the lettuce leaves apart. Put the diced potatoes, cauliflower, peas and carrots into salted boiling water, cook for 3 minutes and drain well. Use lettuce leaves to line a deep casserole dish and then add the vegetables, a couple of sprigs of mint and season to taste. Dot the butter all over and press the remaining lettuce leaves tightly into the casserole. Cover with a lid and bake for about half an hour at approximately 375°F (190°C) or Mark 5.

(4 portions)

SALADS

On the whole, I think most of us look on salads as something to eat during the summer months, but I enjoy them at any time of the year and in particular when I've had one or two rather heavy meals, or with a fairly substantial meat dish.

Salads don't always have to be made from lettuce, tomatoes and cucumber, good as they are, because with a little imagination you can combine a wide variety of ingredients.

For instance, Blackberry Salad is delicious when made in the late summer or early autumn, from cultivated or hedgerow blackberries. As a party salad try Danish Shrimp Salad with tomatoes, shrimps, asparagus, macaroni, lemon juice and mayonnaise. So have a go and try out some of these more unusual salads on the family.

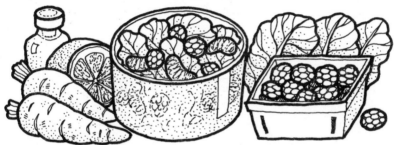

BLACKBERRY SALAD

Ingredients
1 cos lettuce
¼ lb cottage cheese
2 tablespoonsful mayonnaise
2 oranges
1 carrot
· **¼ lb blackberries**

METHOD
Pull the lettuce apart, wash, shake well and arrange on a dish. Mix the cottage cheese and mayonnaise together. Peel the oranges and quarter them, grate the carrot, and on top of the lettuce put alternate layers of blackberries, cottage cheese mixture and carrot. Serve with a dressing if liked and garnish with the orange quarters.   (4 portions)

CELERY, ONION AND BEETROOT SALAD

Ingredients

4 large onions
$\frac{1}{2}$ pint milk and water
1 medium-sized beetroot (diced)
2 sticks celery
2 tablespoonsful vinegar
little lemon juice
6 tablespoonsful olive oil
1 teaspoonful mustard
salt and pepper

METHOD

Slice the onions and cook them slowly in well-salted milk and water. When really tender, drain and chill thoroughly. Mix the onions with the beetroot and add the shredded celery. Make a dressing with the vinegar, lemon juice, oil and seasonings. Toss the vegetables in this and serve chilled. (4 portions)

CHEESE AND MUSHROOM SALAD

Ingredients

6 oz raw mushrooms (thinly sliced)
6 oz Cheddar cheese (cut into cubes)

DRESSING
$\frac{1}{4}$ pint double dairy cream
2 dessertspoonsful fresh lemon juice
1 level tablespoonful chopped chives
$\frac{1}{4}$ teaspoonful salt
pinch paprika pepper
4 sliced tomatoes

METHOD

To make the dressing, beat the cream until it starts to thicken, then gradually add the lemon juice and continue beating until the cream is thick. Stir in the chives, salt and paprika and when evenly blended add the mushrooms and cheese which have been lightly tossed together.

Turn the mixture into a serving dish and garnish with the tomatoes.

(4 portions)

CREAM CHEESE AND APPLE SALAD

Ingredients

2 oz cream cheese
2 tablespoonsful mayonnaise
1 small salad onion (finely chopped)
1 hard-boiled egg (chopped)
1 eating apple (finely chopped)

GARNISH
few lettuce leaves
1 sliced hard-boiled egg
few slices eating apple

METHOD

Blend the cream cheese with the mayonnaise, then stir in the onion, hard-boiled egg, and apple.

When all well blended together, turn into a serving dish which has been lined with lettuce leaves.

Garnish with the sliced hard-boiled egg and the apple slices.

(1 portion)

DANISH SHRIMP SALAD

Ingredients

6 large even-sized tomatoes
5½ oz can shrimps (well drained)
10½ oz can asparagus pieces (well drained)
2 oz cooked macaroni
little lemon juice
4 oz mayonnaise

METHOD

Cut off the top of each tomato and scoop them out. In a basin season the mayonnaise and add lemon juice to taste, then add the drained shrimps, asparagus and cooked macaroni. Mix all carefully together with a spoon. Divide the filling into 6 equal portions and fill the hollowed out tomatoes. Replace the top of the tomato at an angle, so that the filling can be seen and serve on a bed of shredded lettuce. (6 portions)

PICNIC SALAD

Ingredients

POTATO SALAD
1 lb home grown new potatoes
¼ pint mayonnaise or salad cream
salt and pepper
few chopped chives or spring onions

ACCOMPANIMENTS
½ lb sausages
few rashers of streaky bacon
4 tomatoes
small quantity of cooked garden peas
1 small lettuce

METHOD

Boil the potatoes in their skins, and while still hot remove the skins and cut the potatoes into small dice. Mix gently with the mayonnaise or salad cream. Season to taste and add the chopped chives or onions. Wrap one rasher of bacon round each of the sausages and grill until cooked.

Assemble all the ingredients on foil trays, cover, and they are ready to take on the picnic. (4 portions)

POTATO SALAD

Ingredients

6 oz mayonnaise
3 fluid oz yogurt
salt and pepper
½ level teaspoonful curry powder
1 level teaspoonful grated onion
2 level tablespoonsful chopped parsley
1 lb peeled and boiled potatoes

METHOD

In a basin mix together the mayonnaise and yogurt, season with salt and pepper and add the curry powder, grated onion and parsley. When evenly blended fold in the cold sliced potatoes. (New small ones are best.)

(4 portions)

QUICKIE SALAD

Ingredients

$\frac{1}{2}$ lb home grown English tomatoes
2 oz cup mushrooms
4 oz cooked home grown peas
1 oz finely chopped parsley
lemon and oil dressing (1 part lemon to 3
    parts salad oil)

METHOD

Pour boiling water over the tomatoes and skin them. Then slice the tomatoes and mushrooms, and put into a serving dish. Pour the dressing over and allow this to soak through before adding the parsley and peas. Toss all ingredients well together and serve. (4 portions)

SALAD PICNIC LOAF

Ingredients

2 small French loaves
4 slices of ham, tongue or bacon
4 tablespoonsful cabbage (very finely shredded)
2 tablespoonsful cucumber (finely diced)
2 tablespoonsful mayonnaise
2 tablespoonsful double cream (whipped)
1 dessertspoonful chopped walnuts
3 oz fresh mushrooms (chopped)
few drops lemon juice

METHOD

In a basin mix the cabbage, cucumber, mushrooms and nuts, and sprinkle with a few drops of lemon juice. Stir the cream and mayonnaise together, pour over the other ingredients and turn the salad over to blend thoroughly. Stand in a cool place for 15–20 minutes. Cut the loaves almost through, remove a little of the crumb, lay the slices of meat in the base of the loaf, and fill with the salad. (6 portions)

SAVOURY LOAF

Ingredients
1 small bloomer loaf
approximately 2 oz butter
4 oz can salmon
4 oz cream cheese
1 oz chopped toasted almonds
few lettuce leaves

METHOD
Cut the loaf into three slices lengthways, butter well, remembering to butter the centre slice on both sides. Mash the salmon and season to taste, then spread this on the bottom slice. Put the centre slice on top. Blend the cheese and almonds together and spread onto the centre slice, cover with a few lettuce leaves and press the top slice into place. Wrap closely in foil and store in a cool place until ready to serve. When serving cut in ample slices. (8–10 portions)

SOUR CREAM AND MUSHROOM SALAD

Ingredients
3 oz cucumber (peeled and diced)
3 hard-boiled eggs
4 oz mushrooms
$\frac{1}{4}$ pint sour cream
$\frac{1}{2}$ level teaspoonful dry mustard
$\frac{1}{2}$ level teaspoonful grated horseradish
salt and pepper to taste
4 tomatoes
sprigs of parsley or watercress

METHOD
Into a basin put the cucumber, two diced hard-boiled eggs and the finely sliced mushrooms. In another basin blend the sour cream, mustard, horseradish and seasoning, then pour over the ingredients in the other basin. Turn the ingredients over gently with a spoon and stand in a cool place for at least 20 minutes. Arrange on a serving dish and garnish with the remaining sliced hard-boiled egg, tomatoes and parsley or watercress.

(4 portions)

STUFFED CUCUMBER SALAD

Ingredients

1 large cucumber
4 oz grated Cheddar cheese
½ oz butter
1 teaspoonful Worcester sauce
2 hard-boiled eggs
salt and pepper
a selection of salad plants in season

METHOD

Peel or decorate the skin of the cucumber and cut into 1½ in. slices. Remove the centres and chop very finely. Cream the cheese with the butter and sauce, then add 1 chopped egg, seasoning and cucumber.

Blend all well together and place in a piping bag using a large rosette pipe, and fill the hollows of the cucumber slices. Arrange on a bed of salad and garnish with sliced egg. Serve chilled with mayonnaise.

(4 portions)

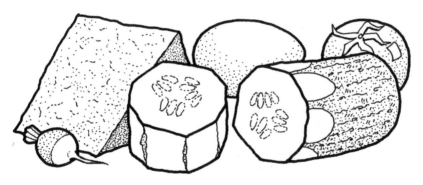

SUN TIME SALAD

Ingredients

3 tablespoonsful double cream
4 tablespoonsful mayonnaise
¾ lb new potatoes (cooked and diced)
1 large raw carrot (grated)
½ lb chicken (cooked and diced)
8 oz can pineapple crush (strained)
lettuce leaves
2 spring onions (finely chopped)

METHOD

Mix the cream into the mayonnaise then lightly stir in all the other in-gredients EXCEPT for the onions and lettuce.

Line a salad bowl with the lettuce leaves, pile the salad in the centre and sprinkle over the onions. (3–4 portions)

WINTER SALAD

Ingredients
**3 rosy eating apples
3 sticks celery
1 green pepper
8 oz New Zealand Cheddar cheese
1 oz halved walnuts
little lemon juice and water**

METHOD

Wipe and core the apples, cut into dice and put in a basin with the lemon juice and water. Wash the celery and cut into pieces of the same size. Wash and remove the pith and seeds from the peppers and cut up. Cut the cheese into cubes.

When ready to serve, drain the apple and mix with all other ingredients, place on a dish and serve with mayonnaise or French dressing. (3–4 portions)

XMAS HOLIDAY SALAD

Ingredients
**8 oz Cheddar cheese
8 oz bacon or ham (cooked)
6 oz peas (cooked)
1 lettuce
2 small tomatoes
sprigs parsley
mayonnaise**

METHOD

Dice cheese into $\frac{1}{2}$ in. cubes. Dice ham or bacon into slightly smaller cubes. Toss together with the peas.

Line a serving dish with lettuce and add the cheese mixture. Garnish outside edge with wedges of tomato and parsley sprigs.

Serve with mayonnaise or salad dressing. (4 portions)

Winter salad, p. 112; egg, cheese and potato rolls, p. 142; savoury plait, p. 199.

PUDDINGS (Hot)

I have divided puddings into hot and cold sections for quick reference, since there's nothing so boring as looking through every recipe to find out which is which. Once again the recipes are everyday ones and most of them I've been making for many years so they are well tested.

In the hot section you will find some good old fashioned suet puddings which are ideal for feeding hungry children and keeping the cold out. My favourite among these is Syrup and Lemon Pudding which I have eaten since I was a child, when it was made by my mother or grandmother.

On the lighter side are Baked Lemon Pudding, Chocolate Crisp and Fried Banana Horns, with their soft creamy filling. These are just a few of the recipes in this section and I hope you will enjoy them all.

APPLE FRITTERS

Ingredients

2 medium-sized cooking apples
fat or oil for deep frying
caster sugar
BATTER
2 oz plain flour
pinch salt
2 level teaspoonsful caster sugar
1 egg (separated)
4½ fluid oz milk (just under ¼ pint)

METHOD

Sieve the flour and salt together in a basin, add the sugar. Beat the egg yolk into the milk. Make a well in the centre of the flour, slowly pour in the liquid beating all the time, until it is smooth. Cover and leave in a cool place for 1 hour. Whisk the egg white until stiff and carefully fold into the batter. Heat the oil or fat to 350°F (180C) or Mark 4. Peel, core, and cut the apples into rings, dip them into the batter, put into the fat and fry until golden brown all over.

Remove them from the fat, drain on absorbent paper, and toss in caster sugar. Serve at once. A little cinnamon may be added to the caster sugar if you like the flavour. (4 portions)

Tipperary pie, p. 149; egg cosset, p. 142; marrow cargo, p. 144.

APPLE SNOWBALLS

Ingredients

6 eating apples (i.e. Granny Smiths)
$\frac{1}{2}$ lb caster sugar
$\frac{1}{2}$ pint water
20 marshmallows
approx. 2 oz desiccated coconut
1 dessertspoonful lemon juice

METHOD

Boil sugar, water, and 14 marshmallows with the lemon juice for 5 minutes, but DO NOT STIR.

Peel and core the apples carefully, stuff each with a marshmallow, and then put the apples into the syrup and cook gently until just tender. When tender remove the apples from the syrup, drain and cool slightly, before rolling them in the desiccated coconut to coat all over.

Serve hot or cold. Any syrup left over, makes a good base for a fresh fruit salad. (6 portions)

BAKED APPLE DUMPLINGS

Ingredients

$\frac{1}{2}$ lb short crust or rough puff pastry
2 medium sized apples (Bramley Seedlings)
small quantity sugar, butter, raisins and
   cinnamon

METHOD

Peel the apples and cut them in half. Scoop out the core and fill with sugar, butter, raisins and cinnamon.

Roll out the pastry to $\frac{1}{8}$ in. thickness and cut into 4 rounds approximately 6 in. in diameter. Place each apple on a pastry round, damp the outer edge and seal over the top of the apple. Turn the apple upside down and place on a greased baking sheet.

Brush with milk and dredge with granulated sugar. Bake at approximately 425°F (220°C) or Mark 7 for about 25 minutes until the pastry is golden brown and the apple cooked.

Serve with custard. (4 portions)

BAKED LEMON PUDDING

Ingredients
3 oz fresh white breadcrumbs
½ pint milk
2 eggs
3 oz caster sugar
2 oz butter (melted)
grated rind large lemon
little lemon curd
2 level tablespoonsful caster sugar

METHOD
Put the breadcrumbs into a basin, bring the milk to boiling point and pour over the crumbs. Set aside to cool slightly. Beat the egg yolks with the 3 oz caster sugar, add the lemon rind and the melted butter, mix all well together then add to the milk and breadcrumbs. When the ingredients are evenly blended pour them into a greased pie dish and bake at approximately 350°F (180°C) or Mark 4 for about 1 hour, when the top should be set and lightly coloured. Remove the dish from the oven, and you will notice after a minute or two the top will sink in – this is supposed to happen. Whisk up the egg whites until stiff then fold in the remaining sugar. Spread the top of the pudding with a little lemon curd, cover with the meringue mixture and put back into the oven to brown slightly. This dish can be eaten hot or cold. (4 portions)

BREAD AND BUTTER PUDDING

Ingredients
5½ slices from a large loaf
2 oz caster sugar
2 eggs
1 pint milk
3–4 oz dried fruit (i.e. sultanas and peel)
Butter to spread on bread

METHOD
Grease a deep ovenproof dish, then put a layer of bread and butter with the butter side down into the base, sprinkle with some of the fruit Continue in layers until the dish is two-thirds full.

Beat the eggs into the milk, add the sugar and beat until evenly blended

Pour over the ingredients in the dish, cover with a piece of foil or grease-proof paper and bake at approx. 375°F (190°C) or Mark 5 for 1–1½ hours. Remove the dish from the oven, sprinkle the top with Demerara sugar and return to the oven at 425°F (220°C) or Mark 7 for a few minutes, until the sugar has melted. (3–4 portions)

CHOCOLATE CRISP

Ingredients

2 oz fine semolina
1 pint milk
sugar to taste (approx. ½ oz)
1¼ oz powdered drinking chocolate
2 eggs
4 oz caster sugar
few glacé cherries
few angelica leaves

METHOD

In a saucepan heat the milk and then stir in the semolina, using a wooden spoon. Stir until the mixture boils and thickens. Add the drinking chocolate and sugar to taste, and stir until evenly blended. Allow the mixture to cool slightly before adding the 2 lightly beaten egg yolks, and pour into an ovenproof dish.

Make the meringue by whipping egg whites until very stiff, then fold in the 4 oz of caster sugar. Pile the meringue on to the chocolate mixture, decorate with the cherries and angelica, and bake at approx. 325°F (160°C) or Mark 3 until the meringue is crisp and firm to the touch. Serve at once. (4–6 portions)

CINNAMON APPLE BATTER

Ingredients
    2 oz plain flour
    pinch salt
    1 egg
    ½ pint milk
    ¾ lb cooking apples (peeled, cored and
    thinly sliced)
    1 rounded tablespoonful chopped suet
    approx. 3 oz caster sugar
    large pinch cinnamon

METHOD
Sieve the flour and salt into a small basin, add the egg and start mixing, then gradually add the milk to make a smooth batter.

Toss the apple slices into the sugar and cinnamon and put into a greased pie dish. Sprinkle the suet over the apples and pour over the batter. Bake at approximately 375°F (190°C) or Mark 5 for about 45 minutes. Serve hot.   (4–6 portions)

CRUNCHY-TOPPED APPLE PUDDING

Ingredients
    6 oz self-raising flour ⎫
    3 oz suet   ⎬ **suet crust pastry**
    pinch of salt
    cold water to mix ⎭
    1 lb cooking apples
    rind and juice of half a large orange
    caster sugar to taste
    2 tablespoonsful warmed golden syrup
    approx. 2 oz Demerara sugar

METHOD
Peel, core and slice or chop the apples, and put them into a greased deep pie dish, adding sugar to taste between the layers. Pour over the rind and juice of the orange, and a little more sugar if required.

Make the suet crust pastry by putting all the dry ingredients into a basin and mixing to a soft but not sticky consistency. Turn out onto a lightly floured board and press or roll into shape to fit the pie dish. Place the pastry on top of the apples and press down lightly.

With a spoon cover the top of the pastry with the warmed syrup and lightly press the sugar all over the surface of the syrup. Bake at approximately 350°F (180°C) or Mark 4 for about 40 minutes, when the top will be rich golden brown. (4–6 portions)

FRIED BANANA HORNS

Ingredients **8 oz rough puff pastry**
4 bananas
small quantity cinnamon and caster sugar
small quantity redcurrant jelly
lard or oil for deep fat frying

METHOD

Roll out the pastry to about $\frac{1}{8}$-in. thickness and cut into 4-in. squares. Peel the bananas and cut in half crosswise. Place half banana diagonally in centre of each square. Brush with jelly or toss in cinnamon and sugar which have been mixed together. Brush edges of pastry with a little cold water, and starting with one corner, roll up and press seams well together. Fry in the hot fat or oil for about 2 minutes until crisp and golden brown. Drain on absorbent kitchen paper and serve hot sprinkled with caster sugar. (6–8 portions)

FRUIT AND NUT PUDDING

Ingredients **1¼ lb cooking apples (peeled and sliced)**
1 oz raisins
2–3 oz brown sugar, or to taste
4 oz margarine
4 oz brown sugar (pieces)
2 eggs
2 oz ground hazelnuts or almonds
2 oz wholemeal flour

METHOD

In a saucepan put the peeled, cored and sliced apples, raisins and 2–3 oz of sugar, and cook gently adding a few drops of lemon juice and 1 table-spoonful of water. When almost cooked, put into a greased 1½-pint pie dish and allow to cool.

In a basin cream together the butter and remaining sugar until light and fluffy, gradually add the eggs and a little flour and when evenly blended fold in the remaining flour and nuts. Spread this mixture over the cooked ingredients and bake at approximately 425°F (220°C) or Mark 7 for about 35 minutes, or when the top feels firm to the touch. Serve with custard.

(4–6 portions)

GINGERED PEARS

Ingredients

FILLING
6 large English dessert pears
1 oz desiccated coconut
1 oz preserved ginger (chopped finely)
1 oz soft brown sugar
little cold water

CRUST
8 oz self-raising flour
2 oz butter
2 dessertspoonsful syrup from the ginger
a little milk

METHOD

In a basin mix all the ingredients for the filling together (except pears). Core, peel and cut the pears into slices.

In a pie dish sprinkle a layer of the filling then add a layer of pears, continue until the ingredients are used then add a little water. Cover with foil or paper and cook for 15 minutes at approx. 375°F (190°C) or Mark 5.

In the meantime, prepare the crust by rubbing the fat into the flour, make a soft dough with the syrup and milk, and roll the dough out lightly to fit the top of the pie dish. Once the dish comes out of the oven, cover with the crust and continue cooking at the same temperature for a further 30–35 minutes, when the top will be crisp and golden brown. The top of the crust may be brushed with a little milk or beaten egg if desired before cooking.

(4–6 portions)

GRAN'S CHRISTMAS PUDDING

Ingredients

$\frac{1}{2}$lb grated butcher's suet
$\frac{1}{4}$lb fresh white breadcrumbs
$\frac{1}{4}$lb self-raising flour
$\frac{1}{2}$lb currants
$\frac{1}{2}$lb sultanas
$\frac{1}{2}$lb raisins
$\frac{1}{2}$lb Demerara sugar
$\frac{1}{4}$lb candied peel
1 lemon (grated rind only)
$\frac{1}{2}$ of 1 nutmeg (grated)
$1\frac{1}{2}$ oz blanched almonds (chopped)
$\frac{1}{2}$ teaspoonful salt
4 standard eggs
$\frac{1}{4}$ pint barley wine
1 oz butter (melted)

METHOD

Grease three 1 pint pudding basins with butter (or a 2 pint and a 1 pint). Beat the eggs together then add the barley wine. Melt the butter.

In a large mixing bowl, mix all the dry ingredients together until blended, then add eggs, barley wine and lemon rind and mix before adding butter. Stir well, then put into basins leaving about $\frac{1}{4}$-in. at the top. Cover the mixture with a piece of buttered greaseproof paper and a pudding cloth, but leave room for the puddings to rise during cooking.

Place the basins in a large steamer and steam for 6 hours. From time to time add more boiling water to the saucepan to ensure it doesn't boil dry.

If preferred, the basins can be placed in large saucepans, in which case have the water level only half way up the basins, and top up from time to time to keep the right water level.

When required for eating, place the basins in a steamer or saucepan and re-heat for 2–3 hours.

LEMON DUMPLINGS

Ingredients

½ lb plain flour
5 oz suet
1 large lemon (rind and juice)
4 oz sugar
1 egg
milk and water for mixing

METHOD

Mix the suet with the sieved flour, then add the grated lemon rind and sugar. Add the strained juice, then put in the beaten egg and enough milk and water to make a stiff paste. Divide the mixture into portions and make each into a smooth round ball. Put each one into a floured cloth, tie securely and boil for about 20–30 minutes.

I like to serve them with hot lemon cheese, but they go equally well with custard or lemon sauce. (4–6 portions)

LEMON SNOW

Ingredients

2 oz butter
4 oz caster sugar
2 eggs
1 oz plain flour
rind and juice of 1 lemon
¼ pint milk

METHOD

Grease a 1½ pint ovenproof dish. In a basin cream the butter then add the sugar and beat again until light and fluffy. Add the yolks of the eggs and beat well then stir in the flour, lemon rind and juice, finally adding the milk. (At this stage the mixture will curdle, but this is quite correct.)

Whisk the egg whites until stiff then fold them into the lemon mixture, when evenly blended pour them into the prepared dish. Stand the dish in a shallow pan of warm water and bake at approximately 350°F (180°C) or Mark 4 for about 35–45 minutes, when the top should be a light golden brown. Serve hot. (4 portions)

RHUBARB BROWNTOP PUDDING

Ingredients

6 oz short crust pastry
1 lb rhubarb
3 oz self-raising flour
3 oz soft brown sugar
2 eggs
1 tablespoonful double cream (optional)

METHOD

Roll out the pastry and line an ovenproof plate or dish with it, then decorate the edge. Wash, trim and cut the rhubarb into about ½ in. pieces, and put them into the dish.

In a basin mix the flour, sugar and eggs together until evenly blended, then pour this mixture over the rhubarb.

Cook at approximately 375°F (190°C) or Mark 5 for about 45 minutes, when the top will be golden brown and the rhubarb tender.   (6 portions)

RHUBARB COBBLER

Ingredients

1 lb trimmed rhubarb
1 tablespoonful water
4–5 oz sugar

TOPPING
6 oz self-raising flour
pinch salt
1¾ oz butter
1 level tablespoonful liquid honey
1 egg
little milk if necessary

FILLING FOR TOPPING
½ oz melted butter
little ground cinnamon

GLAZE
1 tablespoonful warmed honey
1 oz walnuts (chopped)

METHOD

Wipe the rhubarb and cut into thin slices, put these into a 2 pint oven-proof pie dish together with the water and sugar. Cover with a piece of foil and bake at approximately 450°F (230°C) or Mark 8 until it is two-thirds cooked, about 20 minutes.

In the meantime sieve the flour and salt into a basin, rub in the butter until it resembles fine breadcrumbs, and mix to a fairly stiff dough with honey and egg and a little milk if necessary. Place the dough on a lightly floured board and roll into an oblong about ¼ in. thick.

Spread the dough with the melted butter, sprinkle with cinnamon, and roll up as for a swiss roll. Cut into slices about ½ in. thick and place on top of the rhubarb. Return to the oven at the same temperature for a further 10–15 minutes, until it is golden brown on top.

Finally remove from the oven, brush with the warmed honey and sprinkle with the nuts.

Serve with fresh cream or custard. (6 portions)

RHUBARB MERINGUE FLAN

Ingredients
4 oz short crust pastry
¾ lb trimmed rhubarb
2 tablespoonsful water
4 oz caster sugar
1 oz cornflour
¼ pint milk
¼ pint rhubarb juice
1 oz caster sugar
2 egg yolks

MERINGUE
2 egg whites
2 oz caster sugar

METHOD

Roll the pastry out on a lightly floured board into a round large enough to line a 7 in. ovenproof pie plate. Place a double thickness of foil over the pastry in the base of the dish and bake at approximately 425°F (220°C) or Mark 7 for 15 minutes, remove the foil and bake a further 5 minutes to dry out the base. By this time the pastry should be crisp and golden brown in colour.

While this is baking, cut the rhubarb into 1 in. lengths and put into a saucepan with the water and 4 oz of caster sugar. Cook gently until tender. When cooked drain the juice from the rhubarb, and keep to one side.

In a saucepan blend the milk and cornflour, bring to the boil stirring all the time until thickened. Remove the pan from the heat and gradually add the $\frac{1}{4}$ pint of rhubarb juice, 1 oz of caster sugar and the egg yolks. When evenly blended fold in the rhubarb, return the pan to the heat and bring to the boil. Pour the rhubarb mixture into the cooked pastry case. Whisk the egg whites until stiff and gradually whisk in the sugar. Pile the meringue mixture on top of the filling, spread it over evenly and bake at approximately 425°F (220°C) or Mark 7 for about 5 minutes, until the meringue is golden brown. Serve hot. (4–6 portions)

SPICED PUDDING

Ingredients

PUDDING
3 oz butter
2 oz soft brown sugar
grated rind 1 medium sized orange
3 oz black treacle
1 egg
6 oz self-raising flour
1½ oz glacé cherries (chopped)
1½ oz sultanas
approx. 3 tablespoonsful milk

ORANGE SAUCE
juice of 2 medium sized oranges
1 level tablespoonful cornflour
grated rind of 1 orange
2 oz caster sugar

METHOD
Well grease a 1½ pint pudding basin and put a circle of greased greaseproof paper in the base. In a basin cream the butter, sugar and orange rind together until light and fluffy.

Blend the treacle and egg together and gradually beat this into the butter and sugar mixture.

Fold in the sieved flour, cherries and sultanas, and as you mix gradually add the milk until the mixture drops off the spoon when it is given a slight shake.

Turn the mixture into the pudding basin, cover with a piece of greased greaseproof paper, which has a pleat in it to allow the pudding to rise, then steam for 1½–1¾ hours. Turn out when cooked and serve with the orange sauce.

ORANGE SAUCE Squeeze the juice from the two oranges and make the liquid up to ½ pint with cold water.

Mix together the cornflour, grated orange rind and sugar, and blend this with a little of the liquid. Heat the remaining liquid to boiling point pour onto the cornflour mixture, stirring all the time. Return the sauce to the saucepan over a low heat, bring to the boil, stirring until the mixture thickens. Serve at once. (4 portions)

STRAWBERRY CREAM PUDDING

Ingredients   ½ lb fresh strawberries
3 egg yolks
2 fluid oz water
½ lemon (grated rind)
4 oz caster sugar

MERINGUE
3 egg whites
2 oz caster sugar

METHOD
Remove the stalks from the strawberries and place in a buttered 2 pint ovenproof dish.

In a basin put the egg yolks, water and sugar (4 oz) and lemon rind. Place the bowl over a pan of hot water and whisk until the mixture is thick. Remove the pan from the heat and pour the mixture over the strawberries.

In the meantime whisk the egg whites until stiff and then fold in the 2 oz of sugar. When thoroughly mixed, spoon on top of the egg mixture, and if the meringue starts to sink don't worry as this is quite correct. Bake at approximately 325°F (160°C) or Mark 3 for 25–30 minutes. Serve as soon as it is cooked. (4 portions)

SYRUP AND LEMON PUDDING

Ingredients

SUET CRUST PASTRY
12 oz self-raising flour
5 oz shredded suet
pinch salt
cold water to mix

FILLING
1 lemon
5–6 tablespoonsful golden syrup

METHOD

In a basin sieve the flour and salt, stir in the suet and mix to a soft and fairly dry dough with the water. Roll out the pastry about $\frac{1}{4}$ in. thick and line a $1\frac{1}{2}$ pint greased ovenproof basin with some of it. Put two good tablespoonsful of syrup in the bottom of the basin, cut the top off the lemon and then cut it into quarters almost to the base. Open the lemon out and place the cut end into the syrup. Put a ring of pastry on the syrup and continue with syrup and pastry until the basin is two-thirds full. Damp the edge of the pastry lid and put on top, sealing well. Cover with greased greaseproof paper or foil, allowing room for the pudding to rise and steam for 3 hours. Turn out of the basin and serve.

ALTERNATIVE FILLING Using the same amount of pastry, cut a round to go into the bottom of the basin, spread with a thick layer of mincemeat, continue with alternate layers, until the basin is two–thirds full, finishing with a layer of pastry. Cover and steam as directed above. Serve with custard if desired. (4–6 portions)

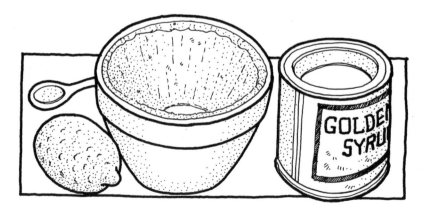

PUDDINGS (Cold)

Most of these recipes can be made in advance which is always a help to the busy housewife, they also help to get ahead when friends are coming round for a meal.

On these occasions I like to get as much done in advance as possible, so that I can spend more time chatting with my friends, instead of working away in the kitchen.

It's very difficult to choose one or two favourites as most of them were made with the ingredients available at the time and with my family and friends' tastes in mind. However, the Ice Cream always goes down well as it is completely home-made. The Coffee Trifle is another favourite because it seems that not many people make a trifle with coffee!

I think you'll have a lot of fun trying these recipes and you will also see how to make meringues if you find them particularly difficult.

APPLE CREAM PUDDING

Ingredients
4 oz packet boudoir biscuits
1 lb eating apples (Worcester Pearmain)
$\frac{1}{2}$ pint syrup ($\frac{1}{2}$ pint water and 4 oz caster sugar)
1 dessertspoonful fresh lemon juice
$\frac{1}{2}$ oz cornflour
2–3 tablespoonsful double cream
1 egg (yolk only)
$\frac{1}{2}$–1 oz caster sugar
1 eating apple cut into slices for garnishing

METHOD
Cut approximately 1 in. off each boudoir biscuit and crush the smaller pieces into crumbs. Peel, core and slice the pound of apples, poach in the syrup with a thinly cut slice of lemon until just tender, but not broken. Drain the apples well and leave to cool slightly.
TO MAKE THE CREAM FILLING Put the cornflour in a saucepan, gradually stir in 6 fluid oz of the apple syrup, bring to simmering point

and simmer for 1–2 minutes until the mixture thickens. Remove the pan from the heat and stir in the egg yolk and cream which have been beaten together. Add the lemon rind and juice and sugar to taste.

TO ASSEMBLE THE DISH Place half of the apples into a 1 pint straight-sided soufflé dish, stand the boudoir biscuits cut side down, round the outer edge, leaving a small space between each. Pour on half of the cream mixture, then continue with the apples and remaining cream mixture.

Just before serving sprinkle the top with the crumbs, and decorate between each biscuit with a thin slice of the remaining apple.　　(4–6 portions)

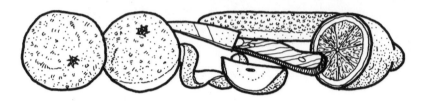

BAKED CUSTARD

Ingredients　　　　　**½ lb rough puff or short crust pastry**
1 pint milk
2 eggs
1½ oz caster sugar
little grated nutmeg

METHOD
Roll out the pastry and line a deep ovenproof pie dish. Put the milk and sugar into a saucepan and bring to the boil, remove from the heat and allow to cool slightly. In the meantime beat the eggs lightly together. Once the milk has cooled, pour this onto the eggs, whisking all the time, then pour into the lined pie dish. Bake at approximately 400°F (200°C) or Mark 6 for about 10 minutes to brown the crust, then reduce the heat to approximately 300°F (150°C) or Mark 2 for a further 1–1¼ hours or until the custard is set.

N.B. A little grated nutmeg may be sprinkled on top of the custard before baking if liked. For a coffee flavour, add approximately 1 tablespoonful coffee essence or to suit taste. For a chocolate flavour add approximately 1½ tablespoonsful of chocolate powder and ¼ teaspoonful vanilla essence.　　　　　　　　　　　　　　　(4–6 portions)

Gran's Christmas pudding, p. 120; coffee trifle, p. 133; norfolk syllabub, p. 137

BANANA AND GINGER CHEESECAKE

Ingredients

FOR BISCUIT CRUST
3 oz butter
8 oz gingernut biscuits (crushed)
FOR FILLING
8 oz carton cottage cheese (sieved)
5 oz carton natural yogurt
2 level tablespoonful liquid honey
3 bananas, liquidised or mashed
juice of $\frac{1}{2}$ lemon
$\frac{1}{4}$ oz gelatine, dissolved in 2 tablespoonful
    water
FOR DECORATION
whipped cream
grated chocolate

METHOD
TO MAKE CRUST Melt butter, remove from heat and stir in biscuits, until well mixed. Spoon into an 8-in. fluted flan ring on a baking tray and press crumbs around sides and bottom to form a case. Cool.
TO MAKE FILLING Combine cottage cheese, yogurt, honey, bananas and lemon juice. Stir in dissolved gelatine. Pour into flan case and leave to set.
    Decorate with piped stars of whipped cream and chocolate. Chill well.

(4–6 portions)

BANANA AND ORANGE MERINGUE

Ingredients

5 ripe firm bananas
2 oranges
approx. $2\frac{1}{2}$ oz Demerara sugar
2 egg whites
2 level tablespoonful caster sugar
1 dessertspoonful lemon juice

METHOD
Lightly butter a shallow ovenproof dish, and sprinkle evenly with 1 oz of the Demerara sugar. Peel the bananas, then cut in half lengthwise and

Batternburg cake, p. 152; Polish cake, p. 160; honey fruit ring, p. 203

crosswise, and arrange on top of the sugar. Sprinkle the bananas with the grated rind of both oranges. Cut the oranges into fairly thin slices, and remove the skin with a pair of kitchen scissors; place the slices on top of the bananas.

Sprinkle on the remaining 1½ oz Demerara sugar, and the lemon juice. Beat the egg whites until very stiff, then gradually fold in the caster sugar, pile roughly over the fruit and bake at approximately 350°F (180°C) or Mark 4 for 15–20 minutes, when the top of the meringue will be nicely browned.

Serve hot or cold, with cream, if desired.   (4–6 portions)

BLACKBERRY FLUMMERY

Ingredients   **6 oz fresh blackberries**
                     ¾ pint water
                     ¾ oz cornflour
                     3 oz caster sugar
                     ½ teaspoonful vanilla essence
                     2 egg whites

METHOD
Mix the cornflour with a little of the cold water.

Cook the blackberries in the remaining water, slowly for about 10 minutes. Gradually add the cornflour mixture to the blackberries and continue cooking, stirring all the time until the mixture thickens. Remove the pan from the heat and add the sugar and vanilla essence. Allow the mixture to almost set, then add the stiffly beaten egg whites and fold into the blackberry mixture until evenly blended.

Chill and top with a little whipped cream when serving.   (6 portions)

BLACKCURRANT PUDDING

Ingredients   **3 or 4 slices of stale bread**
                     1 lb blackcurrants
                     sugar to taste

METHOD
Cut a round of bread to fit the bottom of a basin, then cut the remainder into fingers and use these to line the basin.

Prepare the fruit, cook with very little water and sugar to taste until it is tender.

Pour the hot fruit into the lined basin and cover the top completely with bread. Put a plate on top of the bread, pressing it down firmly and put a heavy weight on top of the plate.

Place the basin in a cold place until the pudding becomes quite cold and set, then turn it out and serve with custard or whipped cream.

AS A CHANGE This pudding can also be made with raspberries, red-currants, gooseberries, rhubarb or a mixture of these fruits.   (3–4 portions)

CHERRY FLAN

Ingredients

SHORT CRUST PASTRY
4 oz plain flour
1 oz butter or margarine
1 oz lard
pinch salt
cold water to mix

MERINGUE
1 egg white
5 level tablespoonsful caster sugar
$\frac{1}{2}$ level teaspoonful cornflour

FILLING
small quantity of fresh cherries
    (approx. $\frac{1}{2}$ lb)

METHOD
Roll out the pastry $\frac{1}{4}$ in. thick, form into a 7-in. round or cut with a 7-in. flan ring. Place it on a baking tin and bake at 400°F (200°C) or Mark 6 for about 20 minutes. When cooked leave on the baking tin.

While this is cooking make the meringue.

Whip the egg white until stiff, then fold in the sugar and sieved corn-flour until evenly blended. Put the mixture into a piping bag fitted with a star nozzle and pipe two circles on the cooked pastry. One round the outer edge and the other nearer the centre, leaving space for some cherries in between.

Bake at approximately 200°F (100°C) or Mark $\frac{1}{4}$ for 30–40 minutes.

When cold decorate with the fresh cherries and serve.   (4–5 portions)

CHILLED APPLE CREAM

Ingredients

2 lb Cox's Orange Pippins
1 oz butter
3 tablespoonsful water
3 level tablespoonsful clear honey
1 level dessertspoonful gelatine
$\frac{1}{2}$ pint double cream
$\frac{1}{2}$ teaspoonful vanilla essence
few toasted walnuts

METHOD

Peel, core and chop the apples.

Melt the butter in a shallow saucepan, put in the apples and water, cover and cook over a low heat until soft. Remove the lid and cook quickly until a firm pureé is made.

Remove the pan from the heat, add honey, and gelatine previously soaked in the water. Stir until the honey and gelatine have dissolved, turn out and allow to cool.

Whip the cream until firm, and fold into the apple mixture with the vanilla essence, until evenly blended.

Pile the mixture into a glass bowl and chill for 2 hours. Decorate with cream and walnuts before serving.   (6 portions)

CHOCOLATE COFFEE CREAM

Ingredients

3$\frac{1}{2}$ oz plain chocolate
3 level teapoonsful instant coffee powder
1 tablespoonful warm water
4 eggs (whites only)
4 oz caster sugar

METHOD

Melt the chocolate in a basin over a pan of hot water. When melted remove the pan from the heat, add the coffee powder and water and stir all the time until the mixture is smooth, then leave it to cool.

In a basin beat the egg whites until stiff and carefully fold in the sugar. Add the chocolate mixture gradually and stir until evenly blended. Fill individual cases with the mixture and chill.

Just before serving top each with a little whipped cream or a tiny meringue.   (6–8 portions)

COFFEE TRIFLE

Ingredients

2½ oz butter
2½ oz caster sugar
½ pint strong coffee
6 sponge cakes
2 eggs
¾ pint milk
double dairy cream for decoration
little grated chocolate

METHOD
Cream the butter and sugar together and gradually add the almost boiling coffee. Mix well and pour over the sponge cakes. When the mixture has soaked in thoroughly, make a custard with the eggs and milk; when cool, pour it over. When cold decorate with the whipped cream and grated chocolate.   (4 portions)

DANISH APPLE CAKE

Ingredients

1½ lb cooking apples
1 oz butter
sugar to taste
2 oz white breadcrumbs
2 oz butter
2 oz caster sugar
little whipped cream for decoration

Peel, core and cut the apples into thin slices. Cook in the butter (without water) and sweeten to taste. When soft whip into a purée. Brown the breadcrumbs in the butter, add the sugar and stir all the time until golden brown, then let the crumbs cool in the pan.

In a serving dish put crumbs in a layer then apple and top with crumbs. Decorate with whipped cream if liked and serve at once. (4–6 portions)

DEVONSHIRE JUNKET

Ingredients
1 pint of milk
1½ oz caster sugar
2 teaspoonsful rennet
1 dessertspoonful brandy or rum (optional)
whipped cream

METHOD
Bring the milk to blood heat, add the sugar. Put rennet into the milk and stir, add spirit if desired. Pour into a glass dish and let stand for 2 or 3 hours in a warm place. Either spread cream on top or serve it separately.

(3 portions)

FRUIT AND NUT SALAD

Ingredients
3 tangerines
1 grapefruit
juice of 1 orange
2 fresh peaches
2 bananas
2 eating apples
2½ oz mixed nuts
4 oz black grapes

SYRUP
2 oz caster sugar
¼ pint water
juice of ½ lemon

Remove the peel, pith and pips from the tangerines and grapefruit, and slice into a serving dish. Make the syrup by heating together all the ingredients until the sugar has dissolved, then allow to get cold. Add the orange juice to the dish, peel and slice the peaches and put these together with the sliced bananas and peeled and sliced apples. Once they have been coated in the syrup add all to the serving dish. Seed the grapes and add to dish, and gently mix all the fruits well together. Just before serving add the nuts and again mix until evenly blended. (4–6 portions)

GOOSEBERRY FOOL

Ingredients
2 lb gooseberries
$\frac{1}{4}$ pint water
sugar to taste
$\frac{1}{4}$ pint custard
$\frac{1}{4}$ pint whipped double dairy cream
little green colouring

METHOD
Stew the gooseberries in a very little water, adding sufficient sugar to taste. When cooked rub through a sieve, or put through the electric blender and leave until cold. Stir in the custard, whipped cream and colouring. When blended pour into individual glasses and serve with finger biscuits. (4–6 portions)

ICE CREAM

Before starting to make the ice cream, turn the control of the refrigerator to the coldest setting. Line a loose bottomed 7-in. cake tin with waxed paper or cooking parchment, round the sides and base, and place in the freezing compartment of the refrigerator.

Ingredients
$\frac{1}{2}$ pint double cream
1 oz caster sugar
$2\frac{1}{2}$ oz plain bitter chocolate (chopped or grated)
2 oz roasted almonds (chopped)
1 tablespoonful crème de menthe (optional)

METHOD

Whip the cream until it is stiff, add the sugar, chopped chocolate and almonds, and, if desired, the crème de menthe. Stir the mixture lightly until all the ingredients are perfectly blended.

Take the cake tin from the freezing compartment, turn the ice cream into it and spread evenly. Cover the cake tin with a sheet of paper, to save ice crystals forming on top of the mixture, and return the cake tin to the freezer.

(This mixture will take approximately 1 hour to freeze on the coldest setting. Once it is frozen, return the control to the normal setting for the time of the year.)

ICED MERINGUE

Ingredients

2 egg whites
4 oz caster sugar
$\frac{1}{4}$ teaspoonful cream of tartar
$\frac{3}{4}$ oz ground almonds
few drops almond essence
a little olive or vegetable oil

METHOD

Cut three 7-in. rounds of greaseproof paper or cooking parchment and lightly oil them all over. Place these on baking tins. Beat the egg whites with the cream of tartar until very stiff. Gradually fold in the sieved sugar and ground almonds as well as the flavouring with a tablespoon.

Spread the meringue on to the paper rounds evenly – you will find this quantity just makes the three rounds. Bake in a very slow oven at approximately 200°F (100°C) or Mark $\frac{1}{4}$ for approximately 2 hours, or until they are dry and crisp, and the paper will peel off easily. These can be stored for several days in an airtight tin without spoiling.

TO ASSEMBLE Decorate one round by making a lattice of paper or thin cardboard strips, and then dust the top with sieved chocolate powder.

Remove the strips carefully. Place another round of meringue on the serving dish. Take the ice cream from the freezer and turn out of the tin. Cut across to give two equal rounds.

Put 1 round of ice cream on the meringue on the dish and then alternate in layers to the decorated top. This dessert should be assembled just before it is to be served. (6 portions)

NORFOLK SYLLABUB

Ingredients
$\frac{1}{2}$ pint real double dairy cream
grated rind of 2 lemons
1$\frac{1}{2}$ fluid oz fresh lemon juice
3 oz caster sugar
1$\frac{1}{2}$ fluid oz whisky
1 oz finely chopped hazelnuts
1 oz finely grated plain chocolate

METHOD
In a basin half whip the cream and sugar together. Add the lemon juice
and whisky alternately, very, very slowly and whip in with a fork.
DO NOT OVERBEAT If the lemon juice is added too quickly it may
curdle. When all the juice and whisky have been added, blend in the rind,
nuts and chocolate by stirring until evenly blended.

Pile into individual glasses and chill for some hours before serving.
Garnish with a small wedge of plain chocolate and/or a small strip of
lemon peel.   (6–8 portions)

RHUBARB CHEESECAKE

Ingredients
CASE
2 oz butter
1 oz Demerara sugar
8 oz digestive biscuits
FILLING
$\frac{1}{2}$ lb early rhubarb
3 oz caster sugar
2 eggs
4 oz sieved cottage cheese
2$\frac{1}{2}$ oz double dairy cream

METHOD
Melt the butter in a saucepan, then add Demerara sugar and biscuits,
which have been crushed with a rolling-pin. Remove the pan from the
heat, mix all well together and press into a greased 7-in. pie-plate. Put
aside to chill. Cut the rhubarb in $\frac{1}{2}$-in. slices and stew VERY GENTLY
with the sugar over a VERY LOW HEAT. Once the rhubarb is soft,

remove the pan from the heat and mash it well with a fork, quickly add the two beaten eggs and stir until the mixture thickens. Allow this mixture to cool, then stir in the cottage cheese and lastly the lightly whipped cream until evenly blended. Pour the mixture into the prepared case and chill thoroughly. If using a refrigerator, cover the top before chilling.

(4–6 portions)

STRAWBERRY MERINGUE

Ingredients
4 oz fresh strawberries
2 oz icing sugar
1 white of egg
few drops of Kirsch (optional)

METHOD
Crush the fruit with a fork adding the Kirsch if desired. Then add the sieved icing sugar and the white of egg. Beat with a good rotary whisk until very stiff (approx. 5 minutes).

Serve in tall glasses, and top with whole strawberries or use in one of the alternative ways given below.

1. Turn the mixture into a cooked sponge or pastry flan case and serve at once.
2. Use as a filling for a swiss roll, sponge cake, or small tarts.
3. Turn all the meringue into one large serving dish and decorate with whole strawberries.

4. Make a no-cook flan case given on this page and turn the mixture into it when set, decorate and serve at once. (3–4 portions)

NO-COOK FLAN CASE

Ingredients   **4 oz rice crispies**
                     2 oz caster sugar
                     2½ oz butter or margarine

METHOD
Melt the butter and sugar together in a saucepan, but do not allow to boil. Put the cereal into a basin and when the other ingredients are melted, pour them over the cereal and mix well together.

Press the mixture firmly round the sides and base of a deep serving dish and chill.

When set, add the strawberry meringue filling .

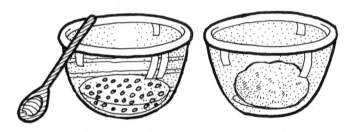

WHOLE MELON DELIGHT

Ingredients   **1 small melon**
                     1 peach
                     1 tablespoonful caster sugar
                     1 tablespoonful lemon juice
                     ¼ teaspoonful salt

METHOD
Cut the top off the melon, scoop out the inside, either with a pomme noisette to make melon balls, or with a silver spoon, and cut into pieces.

Remove any seeds or fibres and put the melon into a basin, add the thinly sliced peach, melon juice, sugar, lemon juice and salt. Cover the basin and leave to chill.

Just before serving put the mixture back into the melon case, put the lid on and serve. (3–4 portions)

YOGURT AND RHUBARB FOOL

Ingredients
**1 lb trimmed rhubarb
1 oz butter
5 oz caster sugar
5 oz carton plain yogurt
5 oz carton real dairy cream
1 oz block dark chocolate
real dairy cream to decorate**

METHOD

Wipe the rhubarb and cut up into small pieces, put it into an ovenproof dish, cover and cook in a slow oven at approximately 325°F (160°C) or Mark 3 for about ¾ of an hour, or until tender. Stir in the butter and 4 oz of sugar.

Press this mixture through a fine sieve and allow to cool. Beat the yogurt, cream and remaining ounce of sugar together until it is slightly thicker than the rhubarb pulp. Thoroughly mix together the pulp and cream mixture, pour into individual glasses and chill.

Just before serving, decorate with the grated chocolate and cream. Serve chilled. (4–6 portions)

LUNCH & SUPPER

What to have for lunch or supper can be difficult sometimes, particularly when some of the family are working and perhaps have a large lunch and others are coming in at different times.

With this in mind, quite a lot of these recipes are quick to prepare and have a short cooking time, either in the oven or on one of the hotplates. I have also used a lot of cheese in the dishes as I find it very satisfying without being too filling.

But just in case you need a quick recipe when the shops are closed, I have included Storecupboard Stand-by. In this recipe I have suggested you serve it with potatoes, brussel sprouts or green beans, but it would be just as nice if served with rice or one of the many pastas available.

BACON AND CHEESE FRITTERS

Ingredients

4 oz plain flour
salt and cayenne pepper to taste
1 egg
$\frac{1}{4}$ pint milk
3 drops Worcester sauce
4 oz minced cooked bacon
3 oz grated Cheddar cheese
little fat or oil for frying

METHOD
Sieve the flour and seasonings into a basin. Lightly beat the egg and add to the mixture, together with the milk and sauce. Stir until the mixture is smooth. Add the bacon and cheese and stir until evenly blended. If the mixture is a little stiff add a little extra milk – it should drop easily from a spoon.

Drop teaspoonfuls of the mixture into the hot fat and fry until golden brown on both sides. Drain well on absorbent paper and serve at once.

(approximately 20 fritters)

CHEESE AND CELERY FLAN

Ingredients

1 cooked pastry flan case
1 onion (chopped)
2–3 sticks celery (cooked and sliced)
3 oz butter
1 oz plain flour
½ pint milk
salt and pepper
3 oz grated cheese
1 tomato (peeled)

METHOD

Fry the chopped onion in half the butter and, when it is golden brown, add the celery and heat slowly. Make a white sauce with the rest of the butter, flour and milk. Pour this on, add the seasonings and the best part of the grated cheese. Put the mixture into the flan case, sprinkle with the remaining cheese, top with sliced tomato, and put under a hot grill until browned. (4 portions)

CHEESE AND MINCE PIE

Ingredients

½ lb thinly sliced potatoes
3½ oz grated Cheddar cheese
½ lb cooked minced beef
salt and pepper to taste
little gravy
¼ pint white sauce (pouring consistency)

METHOD
Into a greased ovenproof dish place half the potatoes in a layer, sprinkle lightly with some of the cheese. Spread the mince on top and cover with the remaining potatoes in a layer. Make up the sauce and put half the remaining cheese into it, then pour over the potatoes. Cover with the remaining cheese and cook at approximately 400°F (200°C) or Mark 6 for about 45 minutes. Serve hot. (2–3 portions)

CHEESE PUFFS

Ingredients
    $\frac{1}{4}$ lb carton of cottage cheese
    1 egg
    pinch salt
    pinch caster sugar
    1 oz self-raising flour
    little butter for frying

METHOD
In a basin mix together the cheese, egg, salt and sugar and thicken the mixture with the flour. When evenly blended put dessertspoonsful of the mixture into the hot fat and fry golden brown on one side, then turn them over and cook the other side in the same way. Drain before serving.
(6 portions)

CHEESE SOUFFLE SANDWICH

Ingredients
    4 slices bread (large)
    4 slices Lancashire or Cheddar cheese
    4 eggs
    1 tablespoonful salad dressing
    salt and pepper
    tomato for garnish

METHOD
Toast the slices of bread on one side only. Place a slice of cheese on the untoasted side. Separate the eggs and add the salad dressing to the yolks and beat until light in colour. Add salt and pepper to the whites and beat until stiff. Fold the yolks into the whites, and pile on top of the cheese.

Bake at approximately 375°F (190°C) or Mark 5 for about 15 minutes, or until they are puffy and brown. Serve at once garnished with thin slices of tomato. (4 portions)

EGG, CHEESE AND POTATO ROLLS

Ingredients
$\frac{3}{4}$ lb cold mashed potatoes
3 chopped hard-boiled eggs
1$\frac{1}{2}$ oz grated Cheddar cheese
4 chopped spring onions
salt and pepper to taste

METHOD
In a basin mix the potato and all other ingredients until evenly blended, seasoning to taste. Mould into rolls or any shape you like, coat with beaten egg and breadcrumbs, and then shallow or deep fat fry until golden brown. Drain and serve at once with hot vegetables or salad.

(approximately 10 rolls)

EGG COSSET

Ingredients
8 hard-boiled eggs
$\frac{3}{4}$ lb mushrooms
$\frac{3}{4}$ lb onions (finely sliced)
3 oz butter
$\frac{1}{2}$ level teaspoonful sage
1 teaspoonful fresh lemon juice

SAUCE
1 oz plain flour
1 oz butter
2–3 oz Samsoe cheese
salt and pepper
$\frac{3}{4}$ pint milk

METHOD
Heat 2 oz of butter in a frying pan, add the onions and sage and lightly fry until tender but not coloured, then turn into a greased ovenproof

casserole. Add 1 oz of butter to the frying pan and add half the mushrooms which have been thinly sliced, add the lemon juice, cook for about 2 minutes, then season to taste. Place on top of the onions. Lay the shelled hard-boiled eggs on top. Make the sauce by making a roux with the flour and butter, gradually add the milk and season to taste. Add the cheese and when melted and evenly blended, pour over the eggs. Cover the dish with a lid or foil and bake at approximately 350°F (180°C) or Mark 4 for about 20 minutes. Grill the remaining mushrooms.

Remove the egg dish from the oven and garnish with lemon slices, paprika and edge the dish with grilled mushrooms.   (4 portions)

HAM AND CHEESE WHIZ

Ingredients   **8 long soft rolls**

FILLING
2 oz grated Cheddar cheese
2 tablespoonsful tomato purée or ketchup
2 oz sliced cooked ham (chopped)
salt and pepper to taste

METHOD
Cut the rolls in half lengthwise and toast on the inside. Combine the ingredients for the filling until evenly blended, and put an equal amount of filling into each roll, then sandwich the halves together. Wrap each roll in a piece of aluminium foil, and leave in a cool place until required. Place the foil parcels in the oven to heat through for about 15 minutes at approximately 350°F (180°C) or Mark 4. When ready for eating strip back the foil.   (8 portions)

HAM AND TURKEY CROQUETTES

Ingredients
        ½ lb minced, cooked turkey and ham
        2 teaspoonsful fresh lemon juice
        salt and pepper to taste
        1 (size 4) egg (beaten)
        little plain flour
        browned breadcrumbs
        fat or oil for frying

        SAUCE
        1 oz plain flour
        1 oz butter
        ¼ pint milk

METHOD

Make a thick white sauce by melting the 1 oz of butter and stirring in the 1 oz of plain flour. Allow time for these to cook, approximately 2 minutes, without the flour browning, remove the pan from the heat, and gradually add the milk. Bring to the boil then add turkey, ham, lemon juice and seasoning to taste. When all is well blended, spread the mixture onto a plate and allow to get quite cold.

Divide the mixture into 6 equal portions and mould into round or oval shapes with a little flour. Brush well with beaten egg and coat in the breadcrumbs. Fry in deep fat for about 1 minute on each side until golden brown in colour. Drain on absorbent paper and keep hot until ready to serve.

N.B. If using these for breakfast make them up the night before and fry at breakfast time. If turkey and ham are not available cooked minced bacon may be used in their place.
        (6 portions)

MARROW CARGO

Ingredients
    ½ a medium-sized marrow (cut lengthwise)
    little boiling water
    little melted butter
    8 oz can baked beans
    1 teaspoonful mango chutney
    1 level teaspoonful dry mustard
    few drops Worcester sauce
    ½ lb large pork sausages

METHOD

Preheat the oven to approximately 400°F (200°C) or Mark 6. Peel the half marrow and remove the seeds. Place in a large baking tin or dish which will hold water. Pour in sufficient boiling water to come ½-in. up the side of the marrow. Lightly brush the cut edge of the marrow with the melted butter, place in the oven and bake for 30 minutes. In the meantime, mix together the beans, mustard, sauce and chutney. Divide each sausage into two by twisting them in the middle, and cut through the skin. After the 30 minutes fill the marrow half with the bean mixture and lay the sausages on the top. Return the dish to the oven and bake a further 30 minutes or until the marrow is tender and the sausages brown. Serve at once.   (3–4 portions)

POTATO PORK PARCELS

Ingredients
    1 lb new potatoes
    4 loin pork chops
    1 oz butter
    salt and pepper
    ¼ lb mushrooms (sliced)
    little lemon juice

METHOD

Scrape the potatoes and slice them thinly. Remove the bones from the chops. Rub four large pieces of foil well with butter in the centres. Arrange the potato slices over the butter, sprinkle with salt and pepper. Lay the chops on the potatoes, cover with the mushrooms, season, add lemon juice and dot with butter.

Tuck foil loosely and securely over the ingredients and place on a baking sheet. Bake at approximately 375°F (190°C) or Mark 5 for about 45–50 minutes. Serve with the juices poured round. (4 portions)

SAUSAGE SIZZLE

Ingredients

½ lb chipolata sausages (with skins)
8 rashers streaky bacon
¼ lb button mushrooms
SAUCE
5 tablespoonsful white vinegar
2 rounded tablespoonsful redcurrant jelly
1 level tablespoonful ready-made mustard
2 level tablespoonsful Demerara sugar
1 teaspoonful Worcester sauce

METHOD

Carefully twist the sausages in two, then cut in half. Slightly spread the rashers of bacon with a palette knife then cut in half. Wrap each half sausage in a piece of bacon, and grill on a medium heat for about 10–15 minutes, turning frequently. Cook the mushrooms at the same time.

While these are cooking prepare the sauce by heating together in a small saucepan all the sauce ingredients. Simmer together, stirring from time to time, until the sauce is of a coating consistency.

Place the cooked sausages and mushrooms on cocktail sticks and serve the sauce separately as a dip. (16 portions)

SAVOURY BATTER BAKE

Ingredients

BATTER
4 oz plain flour
1 egg
½ pint milk or milk and water
pinch salt
FILLING
1 oz butter
8 oz Cheddar cheese (cut in cubes)
½ lb cooking apples (peeled and cut in rings)

METHOD

TO MAKE THE BATTER Sieve flour and seasoning, add egg, half the milk and beat until smooth. Stir in remaining milk and leave to stand in a cold place for at least 15 minutes.

Heat the butter in a large dish, put the cheese cubes and apple rings in when the butter has melted and pour over the batter. Bake at approximately 425°F (220°C) or Mark 7 for 35–45 minutes. Serve at once.

(4 portions)

SAVOURY CHEESE PUDDING

Ingredients
1 lb hot mashed potatoes
2 hard–boiled eggs (chopped)
3 oz Cheddar cheese (grated)
salt and pepper
1 large onion (chopped)
3 tomatoes (skinned and sliced)
1 oz butter

METHOD

Add to the hot mashed potatoes the eggs, 2 oz of cheese and season to taste. In a small frying pan, melt the butter and lightly fry the onion until transparent, then add the sliced tomatoes and fry for a few minutes.

Into a greased ovenproof casserole or pie dish put half of the potato mixture, and spread evenly over the base. Add the onions and tomatoes and top with the remaining potato mixture.

Finally sprinkle over the remaining 1 oz of grated cheese and bake at approximately 425°F (220°C) or Mark 7 for about 25–30 minutes, or until the cheese has melted and is golden brown. Garnish with a sprig of parsley and serve immediately. (2–4 portions)

SAVOURY LAYERED PANCAKES

Ingredients
9 oz self-raising flour
1 teaspoonful salt
$\frac{1}{2}$ teaspoonful pepper
6 oz suet
pinch thyme
$\frac{1}{4}$ pint milk (approx.)
fat for frying

METHOD

Sieve flour, pepper and salt into a mixing bowl, add thyme and suet. Stir until evenly blended and mix to a dry, stiffish dough with the milk. Divide into 4 equal portions, and roll each portion into a 7-in. round. Fry the pancakes in a little hot fat until risen and lightly brown on both sides.

To serve – pile the pancakes on a hot dish with a layer of filling between each one. Garnish and serve with a green or mixed salad.

SUGGESTED FILLINGS

(a) 16 oz can of spaghetti Milanese (heated)
(b) 16 oz can risotto (heated)
(c) Scrambled egg mixed with 3 oz ham and a little chopped parsley
(d) Minced meat or chicken (4 oz) mixed with a grated onion and a small can of mushroom or tomato condensed soup all heated together.   (4 portions)

STORECUPBOARD STAND-BY

Ingredients
1 can cream of tomato soup
6 oz can cream
1 level tablespoonful chopped parsley
12 oz can chopped ham with pork

METHOD

In a saucepan blend together the tomato soup and cream. Add the chopped parsley and bring SLOWLY to the boil, stirring occasionally. Cut the chopped ham with pork into ½-in. cubes and add to the sauce. Cover the pan and cook VERY GENTLY, stirring occasionally, for a further 5–10 minutes until thoroughly heated through.

Serve hot with creamed potatoes and brussels sprouts or green beans.

(4 portions)

TAFFY'S PIE

Ingredients

1½ lb potatoes
2 large leeks
salt and pepper to taste
¼ lb chopped cooked ham or bacon
1 large can cream of chicken soup
OR
1 large can cream of mushroom soup
¼ lb grated Cheddar cheese

METHOD
Peel the potatoes, then parboil in salted water for about 15 minutes.
Trim the tops of the leeks and wash thoroughly, cut in half lengthwise
and put on top of the potatoes, allowing 10 minutes to parboil. Drain
the vegetables, cut the potatoes into ¼-in. thick slices and the leeks in half
then put them into a greased ovenproof dish. Sprinkle with salt and
pepper, add chopped ham or bacon, and pour over the soup. Top with
the grated cheese and cook at approximately 425°F (220°C) or Mark 7
for about 20 minutes. Serve piping hot. If desired, the top can be browned
under a hot grill for a few minutes.   (4–6 portions)

TURKEY SCOTCH EGGS

Ingredients

¼ lb cooked turkey meat (minced)
¼ lb sausage-meat
1 egg yolk
3 eggs (hard-boiled)
seasoned flour
1 (size 4) egg (beaten)
few breadcrumbs
oil or fat for frying

METHOD
In a basin mix the turkey and sausage-meat together, bind it with the
egg yolk and divide into three equal portions. Roll the hard-boiled eggs
in the seasoned flour and wrap each one in a portion of the turkey and
sausage-meat. Coat with the beaten egg and then in the breadcrumbs.
Fry in deep fat or oil, drain, when golden brown all over, and allow to
get cold.   (3 portions)

LARGE CAKES

The one thing everyone expects and gets when they come to see me round-about tea time is home-made cakes, and this usually consists of one large cake or sponge and a variety of small cakes and biscuits.

Everyone enjoys them but can't understand how I find time to make them. Well, it's very simple, I either batch bake at the weekends, cooking the ones requiring a hot oven first and then gradually lowering the temperature to finish with biscuits. On the other hand, when I am cooking a meal I get everything ready for one batch of cakes or a single large cake and just before it's dishing up time, I mix them. Out comes the meal and in go the cakes, which then cook while I'm eating. It's just a question of getting organised!

Here you will find a pretty wide range of cakes and for those people who want a cake without sugar or eggs, you'll find one or two especially for you.

BATTENBURG CAKE

Ingredients

CAKE
6 oz butter
6 oz caster sugar
3 eggs
few drops vanilla essence
6 oz self-raising flour
1 level tablespoonful cocoa
small quantity jam
COATING
1 lb almond paste

METHOD
Grease a tin approximately 11 in. by 7 in. Line the tin with greased greaseproof paper, making a double fold down the centre of the tin. Cream the butter and sugar together until light and fluffy, then gradually beat in the eggs and essence. Fold in the flour and when evenly blended

put half the mixture into one side of the tin. Add the cocoa to the remaining mixture and when blended put into the other side of the tin. Bake at approximately 375°F (190°C) or Mark 5 for about 35 minutes.

When cooked, cool on wire trays, and when cold trim each half into 2 equal-sized squares and sandwich together with jam into a chequerboard design. Roll the almond paste out to cover all four sides of the cake, spread with a little jam and press the paste on to the cake. Crimp the top edges and mark a pattern on the top using the back of a knife.

CHOCOLATE FRUIT AND NUT CAKE

Ingredients

6 oz butter
6 oz caster sugar
grated rind of 1 large orange
3 eggs
8 oz plain flour
1 oz cocoa
1 level teaspoonful baking powder
6 oz sultanas
6 oz currants
4 oz chopped blanched almonds

METHOD

Grease and line with double greaseproof paper a 7½-in. round cake tin. In a basin cream the butter, sugar and orange rind until light and fluffy. Gradually add the beaten eggs with a tablespoon of sifted flour. Sieve the remaining flour, baking powder and cocoa together into the mixture and add the fruit and nuts. Stir all together until evenly blended, then turn the mixture into the prepared tin. Bake at approximately 325°F (160°C) or Mark 3 for about 1¾ hours. To test when done insert a steel knitting needle into the centre of the cake two or three times. If the needle comes out clean, the cake is done. When completely cold, store in an airtight tin until required.

COFFEE CREAM SPONGE

Ingredients

SPONGE
3 eggs
4 oz caster sugar
5 oz self-raising flour
few drops vanilla essence

FILLING AND ICING
4 oz butter
8 oz sieved icing-sugar
2 teaspoonsful coffee essence

METHOD

Grease and dust with flour two 7-in. sponge tins. Whisk together the eggs and sugar, until thick and creamy. The beater when lifted should leave a distinct trail across the mixture.

Fold in the sieved flour and essence until evenly blended. Then divide the mixture evenly between the tins. Bake at approximately 425°F (220°C) or Mark 7 for 12–15 minutes. Cool on wire trays until cold, then fill and ice.

To make the filling and icing, cream the butter and sugar together until soft and add the coffee essence. Spread half the icing as a filling for the sponge and decorate the top with the remainder.

CUT-AND-COME-AGAIN CAKE

– with three variations

Ingredients

3 oz butter
2 oz caster sugar
$\frac{1}{4}$ teaspoonful salt
$\frac{1}{2}$ teaspoonful cider vinegar
4 oz golden syrup
1 egg
8 oz plain flour
7 oz mixed dried fruit
1 oz chopped candied peel
$\frac{1}{2}$ teaspoonful bicarbonate of soda
$\frac{1}{2}$ teacupful warm milk

154

METHOD

Butter and flour a deep 6-in. cake tin. In a basin cream the butter, sugar and salt, then add vinegar, syrup and egg, and beat well together with a tablespoonful of flour to prevent the mixture separating. Lightly mix in the flour, fruit and peel, and finally stir in the bicarbonate of soda which has been dissolved in the milk. Turn the mixture into the prepared tin and bake at approximately 350°F (180°C) or Mark 4 for $1\frac{1}{4}$–$1\frac{1}{2}$ hours. The cake will be done when there is no longer any sound coming from it. Turn out on to a wire tray.

VARIATIONS
1. **FRUIT-SPICE CAKE**
   Sieve $\frac{1}{2}$ teaspoonful of mixed spice with the flour, otherwise all ingredients as recipe above.

2. **FRUIT-CHERRY CAKE**
   Use 6 oz mixed dried fruit and 2 oz halved glacé cherries, instead of 7 oz of mixed dried fruit and 1 oz chopped peel. Add a few drops of almond essence if liked.

3. **FRUIT-GINGER CAKE**
   Use 6 oz mixed dried fruit and 2 oz crystallized ginger, finely chopped, instead of 7 oz fruit and 1 oz peel.

DUNDEE CAKE

Ingredients

6 oz butter
4 oz caster sugar
4 eggs
8 oz plain flour
$\frac{1}{2}$ level teaspoonful baking powder
1 level teaspoonful mixed spice
2 oz raisins
2 oz sultanas
3 oz currants
$1\frac{1}{2}$ oz candied peel
1 oz Jordan almonds (blanched)

METHOD

Grease and line a 7-in. cake tin with a double sheet of greased greaseproof paper. Beat the butter and sugar together until light and fluffy, then beat the eggs in one at a time with a tablespoonful of sifted flour. Sieve the remaining flour, baking powder and spice together and fold into the creamed mixture alternately with the fruit and half of the almonds which have been chopped.

Once the mixture is evenly blended put it into the prepared tin, hollow out the centre slightly, and arrange the remaining almonds on the top of the cake. Bake at approximately 325°F (160°C) or Mark 3 for about 2 hours, using the position suggested for large cakes in the book which came with your cooker.

To test when cooked – insert a steel knitting needle into the cake in several places, and if it comes out clean the cake is done. Cool on a wire rack.

FAMILY FRUIT CAKE (no sugar)

Ingredients

1 oz glacé cherries
2 oz blanched almonds
8 oz dried fruit
2 oz chopped mixed peel
5 oz butter or margarine
5 oz plain flour
¼ pint water
1 small tin sweetened condensed milk
grated rind of 1 lemon
pinch salt
½ level teaspoonful bicarbonate of soda

METHOD

Chop the cherries and half of the almonds, put these into a saucepan with the water, fat, fruit, peel, grated rind and milk. Bring to the boil stirring all the time, then lower the heat and simmer for 3 minutes. Remove the pan from the heat and cool the mixture.

Meanwhile sieve the flour and salt into a mixing bowl. Once the fruit has cooled add the bicarbonate of soda and stir briskly. Pour this mixture into the flour, mix quickly together and turn into a 6-in. greased and lined cake tin, spreading the mixture evenly. Brush the top with a little melted butter or margarine, decorate with the remaining almonds and bake at approximately 325°F (160°C) or Mark 3 for about 2¼ hours. When the cake is cooked, cool for a few minutes in the tin before turning it out on to a wire tray.

To make a larger cake, double the ingredients given above, bake in an 8-in. tin for approximately 2¾ hours at the same temperature.

LEMON AND ALMOND CAKE

Ingredients
3 oz butter or margarine
3 oz dark soft brown sugar
grated rind of 1 lemon
1 egg yolk
4 oz plain flour
12 whole blanched almonds

METHOD
In a basin cream together the butter or margarine and sugar until light and fluffy. Add the grated lemon rind and egg yolk and beat well. Work in the sieved flour until evenly blended and spread the mixture into a 7-in. greased sponge sandwich tin. Arrange the almonds in a pattern on the top. Bake at approximately 325°F (160°C) or Mark 3 for about 40 minutes. When cooked allow to stand in the tin for a few minutes then mark into 8 pieces and cool on a wire tray.

NO-BAKE CAKE

Ingredients
½ lb semi-sweet biscuits
2 oz butter
1 oz caster sugar
1 tablespoonful golden syrup
1 tablespoonful cocoa or 1 tablespoonful dry instant coffee

METHOD
Grease a loose-bottomed 6-in. cake tin. Crush the biscuits with a rolling pin. In a saucepan melt the butter, sugar and syrup, but do not boil, add the cocoa or coffee and mix all well together. Add the crushed biscuits

and mix until evenly blended, then press the mixture into the greased
tin. Leave overnight to set, then decorate as desired.

Suggested decoration: sprinkle the top with desiccated coconut, and
arrange halved glacé cherries in a pattern.

NO-BAKE COFFEE GATEAU

Ingredients
4 oz butter
8 oz icing sugar
little orange juice
1 packet boudoir biscuits
$\frac{1}{4}$ pint strong black coffee (approximately)
1 oz flaked almonds (toasted)

METHOD

This cake should be made on the dish it is to be served on.

Cream the butter and sugar well together, until creamy, then add the
orange juice and beat until VERY SOFT.

Dip the biscuits one at a time into the coffee, drain and place into
position. Spread with some of the cream. Add a second layer at right
angles to the first one, then continue with cream and biscuits until the
packet is empty.

Cover the outside of the gateau with cream and sprinkle the almonds
all over the top.

PLAIN AND CHOCOLATE SPONGE CAKES

Ingredients
PLAIN SPONGE
3 eggs
4 oz caster sugar
5 oz self-raising flour
few drops fresh lemon juice

CHOCOLATE SPONGE
3 eggs
3 oz caster sugar
3 oz plain flour
1 level tablespoonful cocoa

METHOD
(Both cakes) Grease and dust with flour two 7-in. sponge sandwich tins. In a basin whisk the eggs and sugar together until thick and creamy. The mixture should leave a distinct trail across the surface when the beater is lifted up. Fold in the sieved flour or flour and cocoa until evenly blended.

Divide the mixture evenly between the tins and bake at approximately 425°F (220°C) or Mark 7, for plain sponge 12–15 minutes, and for chocolate sponge 10–12 minutes.

FILLINGS FOR SPONGE CAKES

Ingredients

FILLING AND ICING FOR CHOCOLATE SPONGE
4 oz butter
8 oz icing sugar
1 teaspoonful coffee essence
¼ lb chocolate peppermint creams

METHOD
In a basin cream half of the butter and half of the icing sugar together; when soft and fluffy add the essence and mix well. Spread this mixture in the centre of the sponge as the filling.

Cream the remaining butter and sugar together in the same way, and pipe it on the top of the sponge in circles, alternating the circles with a ring of peppermint creams.

FILLING AND ICING FOR PLAIN SPONGE (1)
2 oz butter
3 oz icing sugar
2 level tablespoonsful lemon curd
3 oz butter
6 oz icing sugar
4 oz toasted almonds
3–4 orange and lemon slices

METHOD
Cream the 2 oz of butter and 3 oz of icing sugar together until light and fluffy, add the lemon curd and beat again. Place this filling in the sponge.

Cream the remaining butter and sugar together in the same way and coat the sides of the sponge, also the top. Roll the cake on its side and coat with the almonds. Place the orange and lemon slices in a pattern on the top.

FILLING AND ICING FOR PLAIN SPONGE (2)
3 oz butter
6 oz icing sugar
six small sized chocolate flakes
8 chocolate buttons

METHOD
Cream the butter and sugar together until light and fluffy, spread two-thirds on the inside of the sponge cakes for the filling, and chop up two of the flakes and put these in the centre of the cake. Spread the remaining butter cream on the top of the cake, and round the outer edge alternate chocolate buttons with the remaining flakes which have been cut in half crosswise. Candles can be added if the event is a birthday.

POLISH CAKE

Ingredients
4 oz butter or margarine
8 oz digestive biscuits
6 oz Bournville chocolate
1 tablespoonful golden syrup
2 dessertspoonsful drinking chocolate

METHOD
Dissolve the butter, syrup and chocolate powder in a saucepan. At the same time put the chocolate into a basin over a pan of hot water. Crush the biscuits, but not too fine, then add them to the ingredients in the saucepan. Press these into a greased and lined cake tin approximately 7 in. in diameter, and press down evenly.

Cover the top with the melted chocolate, spread quickly, mark into sections and leave to set about 1 hour.

POTATO APPLE CAKE

Ingredients
2 oz butter
1 lb hot mashed potatoes
4 oz Demerara sugar
6 oz self-raising flour
1 lb cooking apples (peeled and sliced)
3–4 oz seedless raisins

METHOD
Blend the butter into the potatoes, add the sugar and flour to form a dough.

Divide the mixture in half and roll one half out to line a shallow pie dish or flan tin. Cover with the apples, sugar to taste and raisins in layers.

Roll out remaining mixture and cover fruit, pressing the edges well together.

Make a slit at the top, and bake at approximately 375°F (190°C) or Mark 5 for about 45 minutes.

If the top is inclined to brown too much, cover with greaseproof paper for the last 10 minutes.

To make a change serve it at tea-time with cream.

RAINBOW CAKE

Ingredients
12 oz self-raising flour
8 oz butter
6 oz caster sugar
3 eggs
1 tablespoonful hot water
a little milk

COLOURINGS AND FLAVOURINGS
1. cochineal colouring and strawberry flavouring
2. fresh lemon juice or lemon essence
3. 4 level teaspoonsful cocoa

METHOD
Line a 7-in. cake tin with a double thickness of greased greaseproof paper. In a basin cream the butter and sugar until soft and creamy. Add the eggs one at a time with a little of the sifted flour and beat well. When all the

eggs have been added beat the mixture well before folding in the flour. Add the hot water and a little milk to the mixture until you have a soft dropping consistency, i.e. the mixture should drop easily from the spoon when it is given a light shake.

When the flour is evenly blended divide the mixture into 3 equal parts and place in 3 basins, then colour and flavour as detailed above. Make sure the colours are fairly deep, as a little colour is lost during cooking.

Place dessertspoonsful of the mixture from each basin in blobs round the outer edge of the tin, then fill the centre, taking care to contrast the colours. Continue with a further layer on top. Bake at approximately 300°F (150°C) or Mark 2 for 1½–1¾ hours, using the position you would use for a Madeira cake.

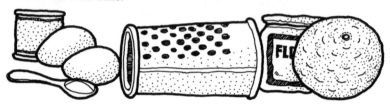

RICH ORANGE GINGERBREAD

Ingredients

4 oz butter
4 oz soft brown sugar
1 orange (grated rind)
2 eggs
8 oz plain flour
1 teaspoonful ground ginger
10 oz golden syrup
2 oz candied peel
½ teaspoonful bicarbonate of soda
¼ pint milk

METHOD

Cream the fat, sugar and orange rind until soft and light in colour. Beat in 1 egg with 1 oz of sieved flour. Beat in the second egg in the same way.

Sieve the remaining 6 oz of flour with the ginger and stir into the creamed mixture, add golden syrup and peel and stir well.

Dissolve the bicarbonate of soda in the milk and stir in, mixing all well together.

Bake in a greased and lined 8-in. square cake tin at approximately 325°F (160°C) or Mark 3 for about 1½ hours.

SIMNEL CAKE

Ingredients

MARZIPAN
1 lb ground almonds
1 lb icing sugar
½ teaspoonful almond essence
1 tablespoonful lemon juice
4 egg yolks

METHOD

Sieve icing sugar and ground almonds, and mix these in a basin together with all other ingredients to a stiff paste. Knead well, and divide into three equal portions. Roll two out into 7½ in. rounds and make marzipan balls with the remaining paste.

CAKE
6 oz butter
6 oz Demerara sugar
3 eggs
8 oz self-raising flour
1 level teaspoonful ground nutmeg
1 level teaspoonful cinnamon
1 level teaspoonful mixed spice
pinch of salt
1 lb currants
8 oz sultanas
4 oz mixed peel
a little milk to mix

METHOD

Grease and line with greased greaseproof paper a 7½-in. cake tin, and tie a double piece of brown paper round the outside of the tin.

Cream the butter and sugar together until light and fluffy and add the eggs one at a time, beating well. Sieve the flour, spices and salt together and stir into the mixture. Add the fruits and sufficient milk to make a dropping consistency. When evenly blended, put half the mixture into the prepared tin, spread evenly and add one round of marzipan. Cover with the remaining cake mixture and level off the top. Bake at approximately 300°F (150°C) or Mark 2 for about 3¼ hours. Allow the cake to get cold, then remove the paper. Brush the top of the cake with a little boiled jam, put on the second round of marzipan pressing it down well.

Make slight depressions in the top of the cake with the thumb to place the marzipan balls in position. Heat the grill and put the completed cake under for a few minutes to lightly brown the centre and the tops of the marzipan balls. Decorate with a confectioner's chicken, or as desired, and a ribbon round the centre of the cake.

THREE TIER EASTER CAKE

Ingredients   **SPONGE**
3 eggs
4 oz caster sugar
5 oz self-raising flour

METHOD
Grease and dust with flour three sponge sandwich tins 5-in., 6-in. and 8-in. in diameter.

Whisk eggs and sugar together until thick and creamy and the beater leaves a distinct trail across the mixture when it is lifted. Fold in the sieved flour.

Turn the mixture into the prepared tins and bake at approximately 450°F (230°C) or Mark 8 for 10–12 minutes.

Turn out on a wire cooling tray until cold.

Ingredients   **FILLING**
4 oz butter
8 oz icing sugar
1½ oz walnuts (finely chopped)
1 orange (grated rind)
small packet chocolate buttons
few marzipan eggs
1 or 2 confectioner's yellow chickens

METHOD
Cream butter and sugar together until very soft. Put a little under half of this mixture into another basin, mix in the walnuts and spread over the top of the largest sponge. Add the orange rind to remaining cream and spread some on top of second sponge. Put second sponge on largest one.

Cut a small hole in the centre of remaining sponge, put on top, then spread the top and fill the hole with the remaining cream.

Decorate the top of the sponge with the chocolate drops, eggs and chickens.

ZENA'S CHRISTMAS CAKE

CHART FOR ROUND CAKE

Ingredients	10 inches	8 inches	7 inches	6 inches
Raisins (seedless)	16½ oz	8 oz	5¼ oz	4 oz
Currants	18 oz	9 oz	6 oz	5 oz
Sultanas	18 oz	9 oz	6 oz	5 oz
Blanched almonds (chopped)	4½ oz	2 oz	1½ oz	1 oz
Glacé cherries (chopped)	6 oz	3 oz	2 oz	1½ oz
Candied Peel (chopped)	6 oz	3 oz	2 oz	1½ oz
Plain flour	15 oz	7½ oz	5 oz	4 oz
Butter	15 oz	7½ oz	5 oz	4 oz
Soft brown sugar	15 oz	7½ oz	5 oz	4 oz
Eggs (L)=Large (S)=Standard	7(L)	3(L)	3(L)	2(S)
Grated lemon rind (ie 1 lemon)	1	1	½	¼–½
Brandy or rum (tbsp)	4	2	1½	1
Mixed spice (level tsp)	1½	½	½	½
Small pinch nutmeg	Varied according to cake size			
Pinch salt	Varied according to cake size			
Cooking time in hours (approximately)	5	3½	3	3

CHART FOR SQUARE CAKE

Ingredients	8 inches	7 inches	6 inches
Raisins (seedless)	10½ oz	8 oz	7 oz
Currants	12 oz	9 oz	7 oz
Sultanas	12 oz	9 oz	7 oz
Blanched almonds (chopped)	3 oz	2 oz	2 oz
Glacé cherries (chopped)	4 oz	3 oz	2½ oz
Candied peel (chopped)	4 oz	3 oz	2½ oz
Plain flour	10 oz	7½ oz	6 oz
Butter	10 oz	7½ oz	6 oz
Soft brown sugar	10 oz	7½ oz	6 oz
Eggs (L)=Large (S)=Standard	5(S)	3(L)	2(L)
Grated lemon rind (ie 1 lemon)	1	1	1
Brandy or rum (tbsp)	3	2	2
Mixed spice (tsp)	1	½	½
Small pinch nutmeg	Varied according to cake size		
Pinch salt	Varied according to cake size		
Cooking time in hours (approximately)	4–4½	4	3½

METHOD

Line the tin with a double thickness of greased, greaseproof paper or waxed paper from cereal packets.

Tie a double thickness of brown paper round the outside of the tin.

Sieve together the flour, spices and salt.

Cream butter and sugar together until light and fluffy. Beat in eggs one at a time, adding a tablespoon of flour with each egg.

Stir in remaining flour until blended.

Mix all fruit together including lemon rind and add to the mixture, stirring until well mixed. Finally add the brandy or rum.

Bake at approximately 300°F (150°C) or Mark 1–2 for the time given in the chart.

To test when the cake is done – push a fine steel knitting needle into the centre of the cake several times and when it comes out clean when wiped with the fingers, the cake is cooked.

Turn out on to a wire cooling tray and when really cold, wrap in greaseproof paper and seal in a container – this will allow the cake to mature until Christmas.

ALMOND PASTE

Cake Size	Made-up Weight
6" Round	$\frac{3}{4}$–1 lb
6" Square 7" Round	1 lb
7" Square 8" Round	$1\frac{1}{4}$–$1\frac{1}{2}$ lb
8" Square	$1\frac{1}{2}$–$1\frac{3}{4}$ lb
10" Round	$1\frac{3}{4}$–2 lb

The above quantities are sufficient to cover the top and sides of the cakes, but as some like a thicker almond paste than others the quantities may need to be varied to suit your personal taste.

ROYAL ICING

Cake Size	Amount Required
6" Round	1 lb
6" Square ⎫ 7" Round ⎭	$1\frac{1}{4}$ lb
7" Square ⎫ 8" Round ⎭	$1\frac{1}{2}$–$1\frac{3}{4}$ lb
8" Square	2 lb
10" Round	$2\frac{1}{4}$–$2\frac{1}{2}$ lb

The above quantities are approximate amounts for 2 base coats of icing plus a simple decoration. If you wish to make a rough snow scene then you will require a little more.

SMALL CAKES

I suppose small cakes were the first sweet things I made as a child and what a thrill to have made them at all, on your own, especially when it came to eating them!

In this section there are cakes that don't need cooking in the oven and so are ideal for youngsters to make, providing they can use a saucepan on a hot plate. Chocolate Bites, Honey Nut Crunch and Toffee Crunch were always favourites with my young niece and nephew and I suppose the best part was when they took them home! So let the youngsters have a go.

Also included are Chocolate Eclairs, Florentines and those tiny Swiss Rolls, all of which are easy to make at home and at least you know what ingredients have gone into making them. Why not have a change and make your own cakes instead of going out to buy them, you'll save money and they really do taste better.

ALMOND MACAROONS

Ingredients
2 egg whites
4 oz ground almonds
4 oz caster sugar
1 oz ground rice
few drops almond essence
few halved blanched almonds

METHOD

Stiffly beat the egg whites, add the ground almonds, sugar, rice and essence. Shape the mixture into small rounds and place on baking tins which have been covered with rice paper.

Top each macaroon with half an almond and bake at approximately 350°F (180°C) or Mark 4 for about 25 minutes. Remove any excess rice paper from the macaroons and cool on wire trays.

Store in a container on their own. (approximately 18)

ALMOND-TOPPED SHORTCAKES

Ingredients

SHORTCAKE
3 oz butter
2 oz caster sugar
1 egg yolk
3 oz self-raising flour
2 oz cornflour
lemon curd or jam

METHOD

In a basin slightly warm the butter, then stir in the sugar, egg yolk, flour and cornflour. (This makes a fairly moist paste, which is easier to handle than ordinary shortbread.)

Divide the mixture evenly between 12 paper cake cases OR spread in a greased 7–8-in. sandwich tin. Top with a thin layer of lemon curd or jam.

Ingredients

TOPPING
1 egg white
1 oz caster sugar
1 oz ground almonds

METHOD

Whisk the egg white until stiff, fold in the sugar and almonds and when blended spread lightly over the filling.

Bake at approximately 375°F (190°C) or Mark 5 for 20–25 minutes, when the top should be golden brown. Cool before storing.   (12 cakes)

BANANA AND ORANGE MERINGUES

Ingredients

2 egg whites
2 oz caster sugar
2 oz icing sugar
1 small banana
$\frac{1}{4}$ level teaspoonful grated orange rind

METHOD

Whisk the egg whites until really stiff, add the caster sugar and whisk again until stiff. Fold in the icing sugar, the mashed banana and the orange rind.

When evenly blended, place dessertspoonsful of the mixture on to greased baking tins. Bake at approximately 225°F (110°C) or Mark ¼ for about 1½ hours, or until a pale golden brown colour. Then leave the tins in the oven with heat turned off.   (approximately 20)

BUFTON SQUARES

Ingredients   **4 oz plain flour**
small pinch salt
1 oz semolina
4 oz rolled oats
1 level teaspoonful bicarbonate of soda
2 level teaspoonsful baking powder
1 tablespoonful warm water
1 oz golden syrup
4 oz caster sugar
5 oz margarine
1 oz chopped blanched almonds
1 oz chopped glacé cherries

METHOD
In a basin mix together the flour, salt, semolina, oats and bicarbonate of soda. Dissolve the baking powder in the water. In a saucepan dissolve the syrup, sugar and margarine, and when melted add to the dry ingredients. Next add the baking powder and water, and finally the cherries and almonds. Mix all well together and spread into a large well-greased swiss roll tin. Bake at approximately 350°F (180°C) or Mark 4 for 20–30 minutes, when the top will be firm.   (approximately 18 portions)

CHOCOLATE BITES

Ingredients   **6 oz plain chocolate**
4 oz peanut butter
1 level tablespoonful golden syrup
3 oz breakfast cereal (rice crispies)

METHOD
Break the chocolate into small pieces and put into a basin standing over a

saucepan of hot water, but remove the pan from the heat before melting the chocolate, otherwise you may overcook it.

When the chocolate has melted, add the peanut butter and beat well until blended. Add the golden syrup and beat again. With the basin still over the hot water, stir in the cereal with a fork until evenly coated.

Spread the mixture into a tin 7 in. by 11 in. which has been greased. Leave until cold and firm, then cut either into squares or bars.

It can be served on its own or with ice cream as a dessert.

(28 squares or 14 bars)

CHOCOLATE ECLAIRS

Ingredients	**1 oz butter**
	¼ pint water
	2½ oz plain flour
	pinch salt
	2 eggs

METHOD

Using a heavy saucepan bring the water and butter to the boil. Remove the pan from the heat, add the sieved flour and salt and beat well. Return the pan to the heat and cook over a low heat for about 1 minute beating all the time until the mixture leaves the sides of the saucepan, and forms into a smooth ball.

Remove the pan from the heat, allow the mixture to cool slightly, then add the eggs one at a time, beating each thoroughly into the mixture.

Using a ¼- or ½-in. plain nozzle (depending on the size you want the eclairs) put this into a forcing bag, add the mixture and pipe into 3-in. lengths onto greased baking tins. Bake at approximately 450°F (230°C) or Mark 8 for about 12–15 minutes for the smaller ones and a little longer for the larger ones. They are cooked when they are golden brown, crisp and light in texture.

As soon as they are removed from the oven, split open one side with a sharp knife to let the steam escape, and cool on a wire cooling tray.

When cold, fill with whipped double cream or confectioners' custard.

Coat the tops with chocolate water icing.   (12–18 eclairs)

CONFECTIONERS' CUSTARD

Ingredients
$\frac{1}{4}$ pint milk
$\frac{1}{2}$ oz cornflour
yolk of 1 egg
1 level teaspoonful caster sugar
$\frac{1}{2}$ teaspoonful vanilla essence

METHOD
In a basin blend the cornflour with a little of the cold milk, and bring the remaining milk almost up to boiling point. When at this stage, pour onto the blended cornflour and return the ingredients to the saucepan. Cook over a low heat until the mixture thickens and starts to leave the sides of the pan. Cool slightly, add the egg yolk and continue cooking for a further minute, then add the essence and sugar and mix well. Cover the surface of the custard with a piece of damp greaseproof paper and allow to get cold, when it can be used to fill the eclairs.

COVENTRY GOD CAKES

Ingredients
12 oz rough puff or flaky pastry

FILLING
2 oz butter
4 oz seedless raisins
1 oz candied peel
$1\frac{1}{2}$ oz soft brown sugar
small pinch mixed spice
$\frac{1}{2}$ orange (grated rind)

METHOD
Melt butter, then add all other ingredients, keep on a low heat until the raisins have plumped and the sugar dissolved. Leave to cool.

Roll out pastry to about $\frac{1}{8}$ in. thickness and cut into 4 squares. Cut each square into a triangle. Put a teaspoonful of the mixture on half the triangles, damp the edges and cover with remaining triangles. Press the edges firmly together and place on baking tins. Make two slits in the top of each cake.

Bake at approximately 450°F (230°C) or Mark 8 for about 12–15 minutes. Remove from the oven, brush with a little beaten egg white, sprinkle with caster sugar and bake a further 5 minutes until golden brown.

Cool before storing in an airtight container. (approximately 16)

FLORENTINES

Ingredients

2 oz butter
2 oz caster sugar
1 dessertspoonful golden syrup
2 oz plain flour
1 oz chopped blanched almonds
1 oz chopped candied peel
1 oz chopped glacé cherries
1 oz sultanas
1 oz chopped angelica
1 teaspoonful lemon juice

METHOD

Well grease several large baking tins. In a saucepan melt the butter, sugar and syrup over a low heat; when melted stir in the flour, fruit and nuts, finally add the lemon juice. Once the ingredients are evenly blended, drop teaspoonsful of the mixture onto the baking sheets, allowing approximately 4 to a sheet as they spread during cooking. Bake at approximately 325°F (160°C) or Mark 3 for about 10 minutes or until golden brown.

Remove the tins from the oven, leave the florentines on them for 2 minutes, then remove with a palette knife. Place them on cooling trays to get quite cold, then spread the smooth side with melted dark chocolate, marking a pattern with a fork. Allow the chocolate to set, then store them in an airtight tin.

N.B. 2 oz of chocolate melted in a basin over a pan of hot water should be enough to cover the base of the florentines. (approximately 24)

FRUIT AND NUT COOKIES

Ingredients
1 medium orange (grated rind)
2 oz walnuts (finely chopped)
2 oz soft brown sugar
2 oz glacé cherries (finely chopped)
2 oz sultanas
2 oz self-raising flour
2 oz corn oil margarine.

METHOD
Mix well together the orange rind, walnuts and sugar. Stir in cherries and sultanas and finally the flour until evenly blended.

Melt the margarine and gradually add this to the dry ingredients. Mould with the hands into 12 even sized cakes, put into paper cases and bake at approximately 400°F (200°C) or Mark 6 for 10–12 minutes, or until golden brown.

Leave on the tins until almost cold as they become crisp while they are cooling. (12 cakes)

GRAN'S BRANDY SNAPS

Ingredients
1 oz butter or margarine
1 oz golden syrup
2 oz caster sugar
1½ oz plain flour
½ teaspoonful ground ginger

METHOD
Melt the fat, syrup and sugar over a low heat. Sieve the flour and ginger into a basin, pour in the melted ingredients, and mix well together.

Take small pieces of the mixture (about the size of a large marble), roll in the hands and press out wafer thin on well greased baking tins. Allow 2–3 in. between each one as they spread when cooking.

Bake each batch at approximately 425°F (220°C) or Mark 7 for about 5 minutes. (They should look golden brown and bubbly.)

Remove from the oven, leave for a few minutes as they are very soft, then gently lift with a spatula or fish slice. Once they begin to harden, roll round the handle of a wooden spoon. Remove from the spoon and cool on wire trays.

Once the first batch has gone in, allow 1–2 minutes before adding the second tray, in this way they can be dealt with easily coming out of the oven.

N.B. As oven temperatures vary, and also the positions in ovens, bake these brandy snaps in the position normally used for small cakes.

(approximately 20)

HONEY NUT CRUNCH

Ingredients

4 oz butter
2 oz caster sugar
1 tablespoonful liquid honey
2 oz plain or semi-sweet chocolate
1 oz rolled oats
1 oz roughly chopped almonds or walnuts
2 oz cornflakes

METHOD

In a saucepan put the butter, sugar and honey, and heat gradually until dissolved. Add the chocolate, increase the heat and boil until the mixture thickens enough to coat the back of the spoon. Stir in the oats, almonds and cornflakes until evenly blended. Pile spoonsful into waxed paper cases, and serve when crisp and cold.   (approximately 16 cakes)

MELTING MOMENTS

Ingredients

2½ oz lard
1½ oz butter
3 oz caster sugar
1 egg (size 4)
1 teaspoonful vanilla essence
6 oz self-raising flour
few porridge oats

METHOD

Cream lard, butter and sugar together until evenly blended and fluffy. Add egg and essence and beat again.

Gradually work the flour into these ingredients until thoroughly mixed.

176

Honey nut crunch, p. 176; picnic swiss rolls, p. 178; chocolate fruit and nut cake, p. 151; coffee ovals, p. 182.

Damp the hands – take a teaspoonful at a time and roll into a ball, coat in the porridge oats and place on greased baking tins, leaving room to spread during cooking.

Bake at approximately 400°F (200°C) or Mark 6 for about 15 minutes.

Allow to get cold before storing in an airtight container.

(20 Moments)

NO-BAKE CHOCOLATE CAKES

Ingredients
4 oz plain chocolate
1 oz butter
2 level tablespoonsful caster sugar
1 egg (size 4)
1 teaspoonful vanilla essence
6 oz plain biscuits (crushed)
1 oz mixed peel

METHOD
Break up chocolate and put in a basin together with the butter.

Stand the basin over a pan of hot but NOT boiling water, taking care the basin does not touch the water. Leave until melted, stirring once or twice.

Remove pan from heat, beat in sugar, egg and essence. Stir in biscuits and peel with a fork.

Pile into paper cases and leave in a cool place to get firm and set.

(8 cakes)

NO-BAKE FRUIT BARS

Ingredients
8 oz digestive biscuits
2 oz butter
2 oz golden syrup
1 orange (grated rind)
4 oz seedless raisins
2 oz mixed peel
little glacé icing

METHOD
Roll the biscuits into fine crumbs. Melt butter and syrup and pour over

Town and country pie, p. 200; cream horns, p. 193; mincemeat pinwheels, p. 194.

crumbs, mix well until the crumbs are absorbed. Add orange rind, raisins and peel and when mixed, press into a greased 8-in. square tin. Press down firmly and level the top, then leave to set overnight.

Cut into finger-size bars or squares and top with the icing.

(approximately 16 bars)

PEEL AND ALMOND COOKIES

Ingredients

2 oz butter
2 oz finely chopped blanched almonds
2 oz finely chopped mixed peel
2 oz caster sugar
1½ oz plain flour

METHOD

In a basin beat the butter until soft and creamy, add almonds, peel and sugar, and mix well together. Add flour and work into the other ingredients until it all binds together and leaves the sides of the basin clean.

Break off pieces about the size of a walnut, roll in the hands and place on greased baking sheets, leaving room for the cookies to spread. Finally flatten each one with the back of a fork. Bake at approximately 350°F (180°C) or Mark 4 for 12–15 minutes when the edges will be turning golden brown. Leave on the tins to cool for a few minutes then transfer them onto wire cooling trays. Store in an airtight tin away from other biscuits or cakes. (16 cookies)

PICNIC SWISS ROLLS

Ingredients

2 eggs
2 oz caster sugar
few drops vanilla essence
2 oz self-raising flour

METHOD

Grease and line with greased greaseproof paper a swiss roll tin about 12 in. by 8 in.

Whisk eggs, sugar and essence together until thick and creamy. When the beater is lifted from the mixture it should leave a trail.

Fold in the sieved flour until evenly blended. Pour mixture into tin and allow to run evenly over the base.

Bake at approximately 425°F (220°C) or Mark 7 for about 10 minutes.

When cooked turn out on to a sugared paper, which has been divided into four pieces. Trim the edges of the roll and cut into four. Roll each one up with the paper inside.

When cold, carefully unroll, remove paper and fill with one of the following fillings.

N.B. To make chocolate rolls, substitute 1 oz of flour for 1 oz of cocoa, leave other ingredients as listed.

SWISS ROLL FILLINGS
Plain Rolls
1. Whip up some double cream until fairly stiff, then add some fresh raspberries or jam.
2. Remove the skin and pith from an orange and drain the fruit, add sufficient thick apricot jam to give a balanced flavour and mix together.

Chocolate Rolls
1. Mash 1 banana, add 1 heaped teaspoonful of finely chopped nuts and 1 dessertspoonful of cream. Mix together and fill.
2. Cream 2 oz butter until soft, add 3 oz icing sugar and beat well. Finally add a few drops of peppermint essence.

BISCUITS

Home-made biscuits taste so different to those bought in packets and they really are very easy to make. However, having made them it's important to store them correctly. They must be kept in an airtight container but not with shop bought biscuits otherwise the packet biscuits will go soft.

Once again you can get ahead with making some of these biscuits since they can be wrapped and stored in the refrigerator until the next time you have the oven on. Coffee Ovals and Pinwheel Biscuits are two such varieties that I usually have ready to pop into the oven when I have finished cooking.

The children will love to help you make these, especially for their own parties and if you are having a few friends in for a drink I find that Cheese and Walnut Biscuits go down very well.

BUTTER CRUNCHIES

Ingredients
4 oz hot melted butter
2 oz soft brown sugar
1 egg (beaten)
4 oz plain flour
$\frac{1}{4}$ level teaspoonful bicarbonate of soda
$\frac{1}{4}$ level teaspoonful cream of tartar
$\frac{1}{2}$ teaspoonful vanilla essence

METHOD
Put the sugar into a basin and pour over the hot butter, stirring them well together, until they start to mix. Add the beaten egg, flour and raising agents which have been sieved together, and lastly the vanilla essence.

When evenly blended leave it until it is firm, then either roll $\frac{1}{2}$ in. balls in the hands or take the same amount out with a spoon. Place on greased baking tins, leaving enough room for them to spread in cooking. Bake at approximately 350°F (180°C) or Mark 4 for about 8 minutes or until golden brown. Leave on the tins for a few minutes before removing them to cooling trays.   (approximately 24)

BUTTERSCOTCH CRISPS

Ingredients
8 oz butter
4 oz light brown sugar
1 egg
$\frac{1}{2}$ level teaspoonful bicarbonate of soda
8 oz plain flour
$\frac{1}{2}$ level teaspoonful cream of tartar
1 teaspoonful vanilla essence

METHOD

Melt the butter and pour over the sugar in a basin, stirring well. Add the egg, vanilla and finally the sieved flour and raising agents. Leave to harden for at least 1 hour. Form into walnut-sized balls, and place on greased baking tins, top each with a small piece of glacé cherry. Leave room for the crisps to spread in the oven. Bake at approximately 350°F (180°C) or Mark 4 for about 10 minutes or until they are golden brown. Leave to cool on the tins, and store in an airtight tin.   (approximately 48)

CHEESE AND WALNUT BISCUITS

Ingredients

3 oz butter
3 oz plain flour
3 oz grated Cheddar cheese
1–1½ oz chopped walnuts
salt and cayenne pepper

METHOD

Rub the butter into the flour and add the cheese and seasoning. Knead this lightly together into a soft paste, then turn out on to a floured board and roll out about ⅛ in. thick. Cut into rounds with a 1½-in. cutter and place on greased baking tins.

Brush the tops of the biscuits with a little milk, sprinkle with walnuts and bake at approximately 350°F (180°C) or Mark 4 for 20–25 minutes or until they are golden brown in colour. Allow to cool on wire cooling trays until quite cold.

(approximately 20)

COFFEE OVALS

Ingredients

3 oz butter
2 oz caster sugar
1 tablespoonful coffee essence
4½ oz plain flour
½ oz nuts (finely chopped)

METHOD

Cream the butter and sugar together. Stir in coffee essence and blend in the flour.

Roll into two long sausage shapes, then roll each one in the nuts. Wrap in foil or greaseproof paper and place in the refrigerator.

When required, slice at an angle to make oval-shaped biscuits. Place on greased baking tins and bake at approximately 350°F (180°C) or Mark 4 for about 15 minutes.

Cool slightly on the tins before putting on cooling trays.

(approximately 10)

DANISH BUTTER RINGS

Ingredients
8 oz plain flour
8 oz butter
1 tablespoonful cream
1 egg white
a little granulated sugar

METHOD

Rub the butter into the flour, add the cream and knead into one piece. Let the mixture rest in a cold place for 30 minutes. If the bowl is put into the refrigerator, cover securely.

Lightly flour a board and roll mixture out into very thin sausages, about ¼ in. in diameter. Cut into 3-in. lengths and form into individual rings. Brush each ring with beaten egg white and sprinkle with sugar. Place on baking tins and bake at approximately 425°F (220°C) or Mark 7 for about 15 minutes, when they should be golden brown. Allow to cool on the tins before removing them.   (approximately 15)

FIVE STAR BISCUITS

Ingredients
4 oz butter or margarine
4 oz caster sugar
1 egg (beaten)
8 oz self-raising flour
decorations (see below)

METHOD

Cream the fat and sugar until soft and creamy. Add the egg and beat well, stir in the flour until evenly blended.

Fit a large rose pipe into a forcing bag, add some of the mixture and pipe on to well greased baking tins, into five different shapes, as detailed below. Continue piping until all the mixture is used.

Bake at approximately 350°F (180°C) or Mark 4 for about 15 minutes, until the biscuits are golden brown. Leave on the baking tins until cold.

SUGGESTED VARIETIES

1. Cherry stars – decorate with glacé cherry.
2. Walnut Circles – decorate with whole or chopped walnuts.

3. Coconut Scrolls – decorate with coconut.
4. Almond and Cherry Fingers – decorate with whole almonds and slices of cherry.
5. Clover Stars – decorate with angelica and cherry.

(approximately 24)

FUNNY FACES

Ingredients

2 oz butter or margarine
2 oz caster sugar
1 egg
4 oz self-raising flour

METHOD

Cream the fat and sugar together until soft and creamy, add the egg and beat again. Stir in the flour until evenly blended.

Using two teaspoons, place the mixture in small round heaps on well greased baking tins, approximately 2 in. apart, to allow them to spread while cooking. Put lollipop sticks (*but not plastic*) in the centre of each one and bake at approximately 375°F (190°C) or Mark 5 for about 10 minutes, when they should be a light golden brown.

Allow to become quite cold before removing from the tins.

TO DECORATE Coat the top side of the faces with white or coloured water icing. Use currants for eyes and nose, a thin slice of glacé cherry for the mouth and chocolate vermicelli for the hair. (approximately 18)

HONEY RINGS

Ingredients

8 oz plain flour
pinch salt
5 oz butter
1 oz ground almonds
1 egg (beaten)
4 level tablespoonsful clear honey

METHOD

Sieve the flour and salt into a basin, then rub in the butter until it resembles fine breadcrumbs. Add the ground almonds and stir into the mixture, then bind together with the beaten egg and honey.

Put the mixture into a piping bag which is fitted with a large star nozzle, and pipe rings on to greased baking tins. Decorate with either a few chopped and blanched almonds or a few chopped glacé cherries. Bake at approximately 350°F (180°C) or Mark 4 for about 10–15 minutes.

When baked they should be golden brown on top. Place on cooling trays and allow to become quite cold before storing in an airtight tin.

(approximately 18 rings)

OLD FASHIONED SHORTBREAD

Ingredients   **7 oz plain flour**
1 oz ground rice
1 oz finely chopped almonds
3 oz caster sugar
1 oz finely chopped candied peel
5 oz butter

METHOD

Rub the fat into the flour, then add all other ingredients. Knead well together until the dough is pliable and free from cracks. Turn the mixture on to a lightly floured board and divide in half. Roll out each piece into a round $\frac{1}{2}$-in. thick, crimp the edge with the fingers and put the shortbread on to lightly greased baking tins. Prick the surface all over with a fork and mark into sections. Bake at approximately 350°F (180°C) or Mark 4 for about 40 minutes. Leave on the tins to get quite cold, then store in an airtight tin away from other biscuits.   (two 6$\frac{1}{2}$-in. rounds)

PARTY SLICES

Ingredients   **8 oz plain or milk chocolate**
2 oz margarine
4 oz caster sugar
1 egg (beaten)
4 oz porridge oats
2 oz sultanas
8 oz glacé cherries (chopped)

METHOD

Break the chocolate into pieces and melt in a basin over a pan of hot, but NOT boiling water. When melted spread over the base of a greased 11½-in. by 7½-in. swiss roll tin and leave to set.

Cream margarine and sugar until light and fluffy, add egg, porridge oats, sultanas and cherries. Mix well together and spread evenly over the chocolate.

Bake at approximately 300°F (150°C) or Mark 2 until golden brown, about 35–40 minutes. Leave in tin and after 5 minutes mark into slices. When cold remove from the tin and store in an airtight container.

(approximately 20–24)

PINWHEEL BISCUITS

Ingredients	**2 oz plain flour**
	2 oz butter
	1 oz cornflour
	1 oz caster sugar
	1 tablespoonful milk
	COFFEE MIX
	2 oz plain flour
	2 oz butter
	1 oz cornflour
	1 oz caster sugar
	1 tablespoonful coffee essence

METHOD

Using two basins, soften the butter, using 2 oz in each basin. Add the remaining ingredients of the plain mix into one basin and the coffee ingredients into the other. Work the mixtures together until each is evenly blended. Lightly flour a board and roll each mix out separately into an oblong shape. When they are even in size, brush the plain mix lightly with a little milk, and place the coffee oblong on the top. Press lightly together with a rolling pin, then roll up as for a swiss roll. Wrap the roll in foil or waxed paper and place in the refrigerator on a smooth surface, i.e. the base.

When the biscuits are required, which can be anything up to a week, cut into slices about ⅛ in. in thickness and place on greased baking tins. Bake at approximately 350°F (180°C) or Mark 4 for 12–15 minutes, until lightly golden brown. Allow them to cool on the tins for a little while, then store in an airtight tin on their own. (approximately 2 dozen)

RAISIN AND CINNAMON EASTER BISCUITS

Ingredients
2½ oz seedless raisins (finely chopped)
3 oz butter
3 oz caster sugar
6 oz plain flour
1 egg yolk
small pinch cinnamon
approx. 1 dessertspoonful milk

FOR GLAZING
1 egg white
small quantity caster sugar

METHOD
Cream butter and sugar until light and fluffy, add egg yolk and beat well.
Stir in the sieved flour and cinnamon until evenly blended. Add the
chopped raisins and sufficient milk to make a stiff dough. Roll out thinly
on a floured board and cut into shapes, put onto greased baking sheets and
bake at approximately 350°F (180°C) or Mark 4 for 15–20 minutes until
golden brown. After 10 minutes remove the biscuits from the oven and
brush the tops with beaten egg white and sprinkle with caster sugar.

WALNUT BUTTER DROPS

Ingredients
3 oz butter
3 oz caster sugar
½ beaten egg
5 level tablespoonsful clear honey
1¾ oz chopped walnuts
4½ oz plain flour
1 level teaspoonful baking powder
few quartered walnuts

METHOD
In a basin cream the butter and sugar together until light and fluffy Add
egg, honey and walnuts. Sieve into the mixture the flour and baking
powder, and stir until evenly blended. Drop small teaspoonsful of the

mixture well apart, on to greased baking tins. Decorate with walnuts and bake at approximately 350°F (180°C) or Mark 4 for about 15 minutes. Remove the biscuits from the tins while still hot, and cool on a wire cake rack.   (Approximately 1½ dozen biscuits)

WALNUT CRISPS

Ingredients   **2 oz butter**
3 oz caster sugar
1½ oz finely chopped walnuts
2 oz self-raising flour
8 halved walnuts

METHOD
Put the chopped walnuts on to a baking tin and place under a hot grill for a few minutes, turning them frequently until they are golden brown, then set them aside to cool.

In a basin cream the butter and sugar together until soft, then stir in the walnuts and sieved flour, until evenly blended. Divide the mixture into 16 pieces of equal size, roll each one into a round and place on greased baking tins. Flatten each biscuit with a fork and bake at approximately 400°F (200°C) or Mark 6 for 5 minutes, then remove them from the oven. Flatten them all again with the fork, and top half of them with the halved walnuts. Return the biscuits to the oven and continue cooking at the same temperature for about 5–6 minutes when they should be lightly browned. Allow to cool slightly before removing them from the baking tins, then place on wire cooling trays until cold. Store in an airtight tin.

                                                                    (16 biscuits)

PASTRIES
(Savoury and Sweet)

Full instructions for the making of the various types of pastry used in these dishes can be found in the Basic Principles section at the beginning of the book.

You will find a wide range of dishes suitable for lunch or supper for the whole family, the recipes are mostly on the savoury side but I find that this is what most people need.

There are a variety of savoury rolls and plaits which are ideal for serving at buffet parties, most of them can be made a day or two before required, then reheated to look freshly baked. These are also good family fillers and can be served hot or cold.

When giving a party I usually make two or three rolls or plaits since it's so much easier than making all those fiddly little canapes and what's more they can always be eaten up by the family if there is any left over.

ASPARAGUS AND MUSHROOM FLAN

Ingredients
8 oz short crust pastry
15 oz can green cut asparagus spears
2 eggs
1 small onion (chopped)
4 oz mushrooms (sliced)
1 oz butter
3 fluid oz milk
salt and pepper to taste

METHOD
Line a deep 8-in. flan ring with the pastry, prick the base and bake blind, using a double piece of foil in the base of the flan.

Beat the eggs until the yolks and whites are just blended then stir in the milk, and season with salt and pepper.

In a small frying pan melt the butter, add the onion and cook gently for about 5 minutes. Add the mushrooms and cook until they are just tender. Place the DRAINED asparagus neatly over the base of the flan, cover with the fried vegetables, and finally pour over the eggs and milk.

Bake at approximately 400°F (200°C) or Mark 6 until the filling is set about 25–30 minutes. (6 portions)

BACON AND EGG FLAN

Ingredients

8 oz short crust pastry
5 bacon rashers (cut in strips)
1 small onion (chopped)
3 eggs
½ pint warm milk
salt and pepper
pinch paprika pepper
3 slices tomato

METHOD

Line an 8-in. by 1¼-in. deep flan ring with pastry. Lightly fry the bacon and onion. Beat eggs, add to the milk and season with salt, pepper and paprika. Put onion and bacon into flan case, pour over milk and bake at approximately 400°F (200°C) or Mark 6 for about 30 minutes or until set. Remove the flan ring and allow to cool on the baking tin if serving cold. Garnish with tomatoes and serve with salad. (6–8 portions)

BANBURY CAKES

Ingredients

8 oz rough puff pastry
FILLING
2 oz butter
2 oz caster sugar
4 oz currants
grated rind ½ lemon
1 oz chopped candied peel
small pinch cinnamon
small pinch mixed spice
yolk of 1 egg
1 dessertspoonful brandy or
1 tablespoonful sherry

METHOD

FILLING Beat the butter and sugar together until light and fluffy. Add all the other ingredients for the filling except the brandy or sherry. When blended together add the spirit and mix well again. Allow this mixture to stand while rolling out or making the pastry.

Roll out the pastry to about $\frac{1}{8}$-in. thickness and cut into 5-in. or 6-in. rounds, about the size of a small saucer. Place a heaped teaspoonful of the filling in the centre of each round. Moisten the edges with a little beaten egg white, fold over two sides of the pastry until they overlap in the centre. Press lightly together, seal the two ends and form into boat shapes. Flatten cakes slightly, turn them over and brush with a little beaten egg white and dredge with castor sugar. Make two or three slits on the top. Bake at approximately 425°F (220°C) or Mark 7 for about 15 minutes, when the tops will be crisp and brown. Serve either hot or cold.

(approximately 9 cakes)

CHEESE, BACON AND ONION FLAN

Ingredients

6 oz short crust pastry
2 eggs (beaten)
$\frac{1}{4}$ pint milk
6 oz cheese (grated)
4 rashers bacon (cut in strips)
1 onion (finely chopped)
pepper

METHOD

Line an 8-in. ovenproof pie plate with the pastry and decorate the edge. Beat the eggs and milk together, add all the remaining ingredients and stir until blended. Pour mixture into the pie plate and bake at approximately 375°F (190°C) orMark 5 for about 45 minutes or until the filling is set.

Serve hot with vegetables or cold with salad. (4 portions)

CHICKEN AND HAM ROLL

Ingredients

6 oz rough puff pastry
4 oz chicken (cooked)
3 oz ham (finely chopped)
3 oz cream cheese
3 oz pineapple chunks (drained)
little milk

METHOD

Finely chop the chicken, and pineapple. Beat the cheese until soft, then add chicken, ham and pineapple and mix thoroughly.

Roll pastry out into an oblong about 6 in. by 12 in. and put the filling down the centre. Brush the edges of the pastry with a little water, fold the sides over and seal the ends.

Place on a baking tin, brush with a little milk and cut diagonal slits along the top $\frac{1}{2}$ in. apart. Bake at approximately 450°F (230°C) or Mark 8 for 20–25 minutes. Serve hot or cold. (6–8 portions)

COUNTRY PIE

Ingredients

4 best end cutlets of lamb
1 lb turnips (diced)
$\frac{1}{2}$ pint milk
salt and pepper
6 oz short crust pastry

METHOD

Trim the cutlets and scrape 1 in. clean at the top of the bone.

Parboil the turnips for 5 minutes and strain well. Stand the cutlets down the centre of a 2-pint ovenproof pie dish, with the trimmed ends standing upright. Arrange the turnips round the cutlets, pour on the milk and season.

Roll out a pastry lid to fit the dish, cut a slit down the centre and put the lid on the dish, easing it over the bones, so they show through. Decorate the edge of the pastry, brush with a little milk and bake at approximately 400°F (200°C) or Mark 6 for 30–35 minutes. Serve hot.

(4 portions)

Mother's fruit scones, p. 216; cherry jam, p. 220; brown bread, p. 211; country style pizza, p. 212.

CREAM HORNS, PUFFS AND TURNOVERS

Ingredients **8 oz flaky pastry**
small quantities of – jam, cream, mincemeat

METHOD

Roll the pastry out to about $\frac{1}{8}$ in. thickness. To make cream horns cut strips of pastry about $\frac{3}{4}$ in. wide and trim one end of each strip to an oblique angle. Damp the shorter edge of the pastry with a little cold water, wind it round the cream horn case, make sure the edges overlap. Place on a baking tin with the cut edge down and bake at approximately 450°F (230°C) or Mark 8 for about 9 minutes, then remove the metal cone and bake a further minute. When cold, fill with jam and whipped cream.

To make puffs and turnovers cut out 4 in. rounds for the puffs and 4 in. squares for the turnovers, place jam, mincemeat, or a savory filling in the centre of each. To finish the puffs damp half the edge and fold over, press edges well together, knock up with the back of a knife and scallop the edge. Brush with beaten egg white or water and dredge with caster sugar. Bake as for the cream horns but allowing 10–12 minutes.

To finish the turnovers damp two sides of the square, fill and fold in half, press edges together, knock up edges and scallop. Finish as for the puffs and the cooking time is the same. This quantity makes 8 horns, 5 puffs and 5 turnovers.

EGG AND SARDINE PLAIT

Ingredients **6 oz rough puff pastry**
3 hard-boiled eggs (chopped)
4$\frac{3}{8}$ oz can sardines in oil
1 tablespoonful fresh lemon juice
1 level tablespoonful chopped parsley
salt and pepper
little milk
little grated Parmesan cheese

METHOD
In a basin break up the sardines, add the chopped eggs and mix together with the lemon juice, parsley, salt and pepper.

193

Potato tart, p. 251; summer casserole, p. 239; orange cheesecake, p. 250

Roll out the pastry into an oblong about 14 in. by 12 in. and place the filling down the centre of the pastry, leaving an equal amount of pastry uncovered on each side. Cut the sides of the pastry obliquely in $\frac{1}{2}$ in. strips and brush with a little water or milk. Plait alternate strips of pastry over the filling, finally sealing the ends well. Brush all over with a little milk and sprinkle with the grated cheese. Bake at approximately 450°F (230°C) or Mark 8 for 15–20 minutes. Serve hot or cold with salad or vegetables.   (4–6 portions)

MINCEMEAT PINWHEELS

Ingredients   **9 oz rough puff pastry**
                       1 lb mincemeat (approx.)

METHOD
Roll the pastry out into an oblong about $\frac{1}{4}$-in. thick. Spread the mincemeat all over the pastry, leaving $\frac{1}{2}$ in. free at one end to seal the roll. Damp the free edge, roll up like a swiss roll and seal.

Cut roll into slices about $\frac{1}{2}$-in. wide and lay them cut side down on to greased baking tins. Bake at approximately 450°F (230°C) or Mark 8 for 15–20 minutes. Serve hot or cold.   (approximately 24)

RAISED VEAL AND BACON PIE

Ingredients   **PASTRY**
                       1 lb plain flour
                       4 oz lard
                       1 level teaspoonful salt
                       approx. $\frac{1}{3}$ pint of water

METHOD
Sieve the flour and salt into a basin. Put the fat and water into saucepan and bring to the boil, and when melted add to the flour and salt. Mix all well together, turn on to a lightly floured board and knead until smooth. Cut off about a quarter of the pastry for the lid and decorations and keep warm. Roll out the pastry about $\frac{1}{4}$-in. thick and line a tin, or mould over a tin with the hands, then trim off any surplus.

FILLING
¾ lb veal (when trimmed) breast and neck cuts
¾ lb thick bacon rashers
1 level teaspoonful chopped parsley
salt and pepper
grated rind of 1 lemon
1 dessertspoonful lemon juice
2 hard-boiled eggs
small pinch ground nutmeg
1 pig's trotter (for jelly stock)
little beaten egg

METHOD
In a basin mix all the ingredients together once the veal and bacon have
been cut into ¼-in. cubes; except for the eggs, beaten egg and jelly stock.
Once evenly blended add a little stock to moisten the ingredients. Fill the
pastry case to within ½ in. of the top, add the whole eggs between the
meat. Roll out the lid, damp the edge, and press firmly on the inside of
the pastry case. Crimp the edge and decorate with pastry leaves, also
make a hole in the centre of the pie. Place the pie on a baking sheet and
cook for about 45 minutes at approximately 425°F (220°C) or Mark 7.
Remove from the oven, and also from the tin, brush all over the outside
with beaten egg, place on a baking sheet and return to the oven for a
further 45 minutes at the same temperature, covering the top with greaseproof paper if it gets too brown.

Once this pie is cooked, strain the stock from the trotter and fill the
pie with stock through the hole in the middle of the pie, continue filling
until no more stock can be added. The pie must not be eaten until quite
cold. (6–8 portions)

ROUGH PUFF PASTRY

Ingredients   **1 lb plain flour
pinch salt
6 oz lard
6 oz margarine
approx. 8 fluid oz cold water**

METHOD
Sieve the flour and salt together into a basin. Add the fat and cut with a
round-bladed knife into small even-sized pieces. Add most of the water

and mix the paste using the knife, add the remaining water gradually until the paste clings together and leaves the sides of the basin clean. Turn the paste out on to a floured board, and roll into a long strip. Fold the top third down and the bottom third up, so that the paste is folded into three. Press the open edges together with the fingers or a rolling pin, quarter turn the pastry and roll out again into a strip. Fold in three and repeat the process again a further three times. It is then ready for use.   (makes 1 lb)

DISHES MADE WITH THE 1 LB OF PASTRY
1. Plate Pie – 7–8 in. in diameter
2. 1 dozen mincepies
3. 1 dozen marmincepies (using 2 tablespoonsful of marmalade mixed with 2 tablespoonsful of mincemeat)
4. 6 cream horns
5. 14 sardine and cheese rolls

TO MAKE THE SARDINE AND CHEESE ROLLS Roll the pastry out, brush with beaten egg, sprinkle all over with Parmesan cheese, place halved sardines in rows and roll up as for sausage rolls. Brush with egg before baking, at approximately 450°F (230°C) or Mark 8 for about 10 minutes.

N.B. I use the above temperature for cooking all rough puff pastry dishes, varying their position in the oven according to their density.

SALMON AND ASPARAGUS FLANS

Ingredients

FLAN BASE
4 oz plain flour
pinch salt
pinch cayenne pepper
2 oz margarine
2 oz cheese (finely grated)
water to mix

FILLING
7½ oz can salmon
6 asparagus spears
1 egg
2½ fluid oz milk
pepper

METHOD

Sieve flour, salt and cayenne together, rub in fat until it resembles fine breadcrumbs. Stir in cheese. Mix to a firm but pliable dough with the water. Divide into 4 equal portions and roll each piece to fit a 4-hole Yorkshire pudding pan. Lightly mash the salmon, stir in sliced asparagus, add beaten egg and milk and season.

Pour into pastry cases and bake at approximately 425°F (220°C) or Mark 7 for about 25 minutes or until the pastry and filling are golden brown. Allow to cool slightly in the pans before removing, otherwise they could break. (4 portions)

SARDINE, EGG AND TOMATO PIE

Ingredients

6 oz rough puff pastry
4 oz can sardines in oil
2 hard-boiled eggs
3 small tomatoes (skinned and sliced)
few drops lemon juice

METHOD

Roll out a little under half of the pastry and line a 7-in.–8-in. ovenproof plate. Drain the sardines and break up with a fork, then spread over the pastry. Sprinkle on the drops of lemon juice, slice the eggs and lay on top of the sardines and the tomatoes on top of the eggs. Roll out the remaining pastry and cover the pie. Seal the edges, decorate and make two or three slits in the centre of the top. Lightly brush with a little milk and bake at approximately 425°F (220°C) or Mark 7 for about 25–30 minutes. Serve either hot or cold. (6–8 portions)

SAUSAGE, APPLE AND ONION ROLL

Ingredients

8 oz rough puff pastry
¾ lb sausage meat (pork)
2 Granny Smith apples (peeled and chopped)
1 medium sized onion (chopped)
salt and pepper
½ level teaspoonful sage

Roll the pastry out into an oblong about 10 in. by 8 in.

Mix the sausage meat, apples, onion and sage together and season with the salt and pepper to taste. When thoroughly mixed put in a roll down the centre of the pastry. Brush the edges of the pastry with a little milk,, then taking the two long sides, fold up until they meet in the centre. Crimp the top edge of the roll, and seal the ends. Brush all over with a little milk and then make several slits in the roll on either side of the crimping.

Place on a baking sheet and bake at approximately 425°F (220°C) or Mark 7 for about 25–30 minutes or until golden brown all over. Serve either hot or cold.   (6–8 portions)

SAVOURY BACON ROLL

Ingredients   **8 oz rough puff pastry**
¼ lb mushrooms (finely chopped)
4 small tomatoes (skinned and finely chopped)
4 rashers of lean bacon
salt and pepper

METHOD

Remove the rind from the bacon. In a basin mix together the tomatoes and mushrooms with seasoning to taste. Roll out the pastry into an oblong approximately 12 in. by 8 in. Lay the rashers of bacon on the pastry, and spread over the savoury mixture. Moisten the outside edge of the pastry, all the way round, roll up like a roly-poly, and seal the ends well. Place the roll on a baking sheet, make several cuts in the top of the roll to allow the steam to escape. Brush with a little beaten egg and bake at approximately 425°F (220°C) or Mark 7 for about 45 minutes. Serve hot with gravy and extra vegetables if desired.   (6 portions)

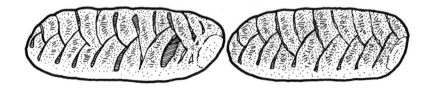

SAVOURY PLAIT

Ingredients
$\frac{1}{2}$ lb streaky bacon (minced)
2 oz mushrooms (chopped)
1 oz onion (chopped)
$\frac{1}{4}$ pint thick white sauce
1 hard-boiled egg (chopped)
1 level dessertspoonful parsley (chopped)
pinch nutmeg
$\frac{1}{2}$ lb rough puff pastry

METHOD
Cook bacon, mushrooms and onion very gently together for about 8 minutes. Stir in the sauce, egg, parsley and nutmeg and mix well together. Turn mixture out on to a plate and allow to get cold.

Roll out the pastry into an oblong approximately 10 in. by 8 in. Place the filling down the centre of the pastry, leaving an equal amount of pastry visible on each side. Cut this obliquely in $\frac{1}{2}$-in. strips.

Fold the ends of the roll in, then plait alternate strips of pastry over the top of the filling. Place on a baking tin, brush with beaten egg or milk and bake at approximately 425°F (220°C) or Mark 7 for 25–30 minutes.

Serve hot or cold.   (8 portions)

STEAK, BACON AND MUSHROOM PIE

Ingredients
TOPPING
4 oz rough puff pastry OR a small quantity of hot mashed potato

FILLING
1 oz white fat
1 small onion (peeled and chopped)
2 oz streaky bacon (cut in small pieces)
2 oz mushrooms (sliced)
$\frac{3}{4}$ lb stewing steak (cut into $\frac{1}{4}$-in. cubes)
7 fluid oz stock or tomato juice
1 small teaspoonful dry mustard
salt and pepper to taste

METHOD

If using pastry roll out and cut a top for the dish. When using mashed potatoes prepare these while the filling is cooking.

In a frying pan melt the fat and cook the onion and bacon for 2–3 minutes. Toss the steak in seasoned flour and add to the pan, frying lightly, then add the mushrooms. After 2–3 minutes add the remaining ingredients and simmer for about 45 minutes or until the meat is tender.

Pour the ingredients into a heatproof pie dish, cover with the pastry lid and bake at approximately 425°F (220°C) or Mark 7 for about 25 minutes.

Alternatively pipe on the mashed potatoes in a pattern, in both cases brush the top with a little milk and make a hole for the steam to escape.

(2–3 portions)

TOWN AND COUNTRY PIE

Ingredients

10 oz short crust pastry
6 oz streaky bacon
2 oz fresh mushrooms (sliced)
4 eggs
small pinch herbs
salt and pepper
2 oz grated Cheddar cheese

METHOD

Trim the bacon and cut into thin strips. Line two deep foil plates 6 in. in diameter with half the pastry. Into this put the bacon, mushrooms and herbs. Make small hollows in the mixture and break one egg into each, sprinkle with salt, pepper and cheese.

Cover the dishes with the remaining pastry, decorating the tops from the scraps. Make a hole in the centre of the pies, brush with egg or milk and bake at approximately 425°F (220°C) or Mark 7 for about 40 minutes.

Serve with vegetables in winter and a salad in summer.   (4 portions)

FRUIT LOAVES

Most of these recipes have two uses – one as a cake, cut and eaten just as it is and secondly as fruit bread which can be spread with butter and therefore helps to ring the changes with plain bread and butter.

You will also find them useful if you have to pack up lunch boxes for the family, so make two at a time to fill the oven and then this will give you one in cut and one to keep.

Some of the loaves have toppings or icings, so if you are really too busy to make a large cake for tea, these would serve just as well. They keep very well in an airtight tin, providing the family doesn't know where it is, they also make a perfect gift for an elderly person living on their own, as they are tasty and nutritious.

BANANA AND NUT LOAF

Ingredients

3 oz butter
6 oz caster sugar
2 eggs
10 oz skinned bananas
8 oz plain flour
3 level teaspoonsful baking powder
$\frac{1}{2}$ level teaspoonful salt
2 oz coarsely chopped walnuts

METHOD
In a basin cream the butter until soft, work in the sugar and add the eggs one at a time and beat the mixture until smooth.

Mash the bananas well with a fork, then add to the egg mixture and beat until evenly blended.

Sieve together the flour, baking powder and salt, add to the egg mixture except for 1 tablespoonful, stir until the flour has been worked into the mixture. Stir the remaining flour into the nuts and add to the mixture. When all blended together turn the mixture into a well greased 2-lb loaf tin and bake at approximately 350°F (180°C) or Mark 4 for 1 hour to 1¼ hours. When firm to the touch, turn the loaf out of the tin, cool on a wire cooling tray and serve as it is or spread with butter.

DATE AND WALNUT LOAVES

Ingredients

1 lb self-raising flour
$\frac{1}{2}$ level teaspoonful salt
$\frac{1}{2}$ level teaspoonful mixed spice
2 oz caster sugar
6 oz dates (chopped)
2 oz walnuts (finely chopped)
scant $\frac{1}{2}$ pint milk
4 level tablespoonsful malt extract
4 level tablespoonsful golden syrup

Tins used

2 loaf tins measuring 9 in. by 5 in. by $2\frac{5}{8}$ in.

METHOD

Line the loaf tins with greased greaseproof paper. Into a basin sieve the flour, salt and spice, add the sugar, dates and nuts and stir until evenly mixed.

In the meantime, heat in a saucepan the milk, malt extract and syrup, gently, and when evenly blended pour into the dry ingredients. Beat well for about 1 minute, then divide the mixture evenly between the prepared tins, levelling the top with a knife. Place the tins side by side on the same shelf in the oven.

Bake at approximately 350°F (180°C) or Mark 4 for about 1 hour, when the top should be firm to the touch and the loaf has started to shrink away from the sides of the tin.

Turn out on to a wire cooling tray and allow to get quite cold, then store in an airtight tin. To serve slice and spread with butter, or as a change, after several days, toast and spread with butter.

FRUIT AND WALNUT LOAF

Ingredients

FILLING AND TOPPING
2 oz Demerara sugar
2 oz walnuts (finely chopped)
$\frac{1}{2}$ level teaspoonful ground cinnamon
$\frac{1}{2}$ oz melted butter
LOAF
10 oz self-raising flour
2 oz butter
4 oz seedless raisins
2 eggs (size 4)
$\frac{1}{4}$ pint (less 1 tablespoonful) milk
4 oz black treacle

METHOD

Mix together all the ingredients for the filling and topping.

Sieve the flour into a basin and rub in the butter until it resembles fine breadcrumbs, add the raisins. Beat the eggs together and blend into the milk and treacle. When blended pour into the flour and mix lightly together. Put half the loaf mixture into a greased and lined 2-lb loaf tin, sprinkle on half of the filling and topping mixture, add the remaining loaf mixture and finally top off with the topping. Bake at approximately 350°F (180°C) or Mark 4 for about 1 hour. When cooked remove the loaf from the tin and cool on a wire tray. Store in an airtight tin.

HONEY FRUIT RING

Ingredients

1 lb self-raising flour
pinch salt
4 oz butter or margarine
3 oz caster sugar
3 eggs
approx. 2 tablespoonsful milk
FILLING
2 medium-sized Bramley apples (peeled, cored and chopped)
2 tablespoonsful clear honey (warmed)
4 oz mixed dried fruit
2 oz mixed candied peel (chopped)

In a basin sieve the flour and salt, rub in the butter or margarine until it resembles fine breadcrumbs, then add the sugar. Lightly beat the eggs, add to the mixture and make into a dough with a little milk. The dough should be fairly stiff when ready for use.

Roll out the mixture, on a lightly floured board, into an oblong about $\frac{1}{4}$ in. thick. Spread the honey on the mixture leaving about 1 in. round the outer edge.

Mix together the fruit, peel and apples, sprinkle evenly over the honey, moisten edges of the mixture and roll up like a swiss roll, starting at one of the longer edges. Twist into a ring, moisten the ends with a little water, and press well together.

Lift the ring on to a greased baking sheet, and snip half-way through with scissors in several places. Bake at approximately 425°F (220°C) or Mark 7 for 20–25 minutes. When cold serve in slices with butter.

MALT FRUIT LOAF

Ingredients

8 oz self-raising flour
4 oz seedless raisins or sultanas
1 level tablespoonful malt extract
1 rounded tablespoonful golden syrup
1 teaspoonful caster sugar (rounded)
4 fluid oz milk

METHOD

Grease and line with greased greaseproof paper a 1-lb loaf tin. In a basin put the sieved flour and sugar, add the fruit and mix well together. In a saucepan melt over a low heat the malt extract and syrup.

Pour this into the flour mixture together with about $\frac{3}{4}$ of the milk, stir well together and finally add the remaining milk, if necessary. The dough should be fairly soft when mixed.

Turn the mixture into the prepared tin, level the top and bake at approximately 325°F (170°C) or Mark 3 for about 50 minutes to 1 hour. Remove from the tin when baked and allow to cool on a wire cooling rack. When cold slice and spread with butter.

MALTED FRUIT LOAF

Ingredients
8 oz self-raising flour
4 oz dried fruit (currants, sultanas and raisins)
2 oz caster sugar
2 oz malted milk crystals (Bournvita type)
2 tablespoonful warmed golden syrup
approx. ¼ pint milk and water

METHOD
Into a basin sieve the flour, then add sugar, crystals and dried fruit. Mix all well together.

Add the warmed syrup and enough milk to form a soft dropping consistency.

Pour into a 1-lb greased or greased and lined loaf tin and bake at approximately 350°F (180°C) or Mark 4 for about 1 hour when the top of the loaf will be firm to the touch.

MALTED FRUIT AND WALNUT LOAF

Ingredients
6 oz dates or raisins (stoned and chopped)
1 level teaspoonful bicarbonate of soda
⅓ pint boiling water
2 oz butter or margarine
4 oz caster sugar
2 level dessertspoonsful malted milk powder
   (Horlicks type)
1 egg (beaten)
12 oz self-raising flour
1 level teaspoonful baking powder
1 drop vanilla essence
2 oz walnuts (chopped)

METHOD

Grease and line the base of a 2-lb loaf tin with greaseproof paper. Into a basin put the dates and bicarbonate of soda, pour on the boiling water and leave to cool, stirring occasionally. Cream butter, mix sugar and malted milk powder together, add to butter and continue creaming until light and fluffy. Add egg gradually. Sieve flour and baking powder together and gradually add to the creamed mixture alternately with the date mixture. Finally add the vanilla essence and walnuts and mix all well together. Put the mixture into the prepared tin and bake at approximately 325°F (170°C) or Mark 3 for about 1½ hours. Remove from the tin when done and leave to get cold on a cooling tray. Spread with butter and serve.

ORANGE LOAF

Ingredients

2 oz butter
6 oz caster sugar
1 egg (beaten)
½ large orange (grated rind)
3 tablespoonsful orange juice
2 tablespoonsful milk
7 oz self-raising flour
large pinch salt

METHOD

Grease and line a 2-lb loaf tin with greased greaseproof paper. Cream the butter until very soft and then work in the sugar until evenly blended. Add the egg and beat, also the milk and orange rind.

Sieve the flour and salt into the mixture and stir in, adding the orange juice as you go. Put the mixture into the prepared tin and spread evenly on the top. Bake at approximately 375°F (190°C) or Mark 5 for 50 minutes to 1 hour, when the loaf should have started to shrink from the sides of the tin. Turn out and cool on a wire tray.

PEEL AND NUT LOAVES

Ingredients
     1½ lb self-raising flour
1 level teaspoonful salt
6 oz caster sugar
4 oz candied peel
3 oz walnuts (finely chopped)
4 eggs (size 4)
scant pint milk
4 oz butter (melted)

Tins used
     2 loaf tins measuring 9 in. by 5 in. by 2⅝ in.

METHOD
Line the loaf tins with greased greaseproof paper.

Into a basin sieve the flour and salt, then add the sugar, peel and walnuts and stir until evenly mixed.

Lightly beat the eggs into the milk then add to the dry ingredients, stirring well until the mixture is evenly blended. Finally fold in the melted butter, until no traces of the butter can be seen. Divide the mixture evenly between the two tins and level off the top. Place the tins side by side on the same shelf in the oven. Bake at approximately 350°F (180°C) or Mark 4 for 1–1¼ hours, when the tops should be firm to the touch and the loaf has started to shrink away from the sides of the tin.

Turn out on to a wire cooling tray and allow to get quite cold, then store in an airtight tin. To serve, slice and spread with butter.

PINEAPPLE AND NUT LOAF

Ingredients
     8 oz can pineapple pieces (chopped)
2 oz walnuts (chopped)
4 oz butter
2 oz caster sugar
3 level tablespoonsful black treacle
1 egg
12 oz self-raising flour
ICING
3 oz icing sugar
1 tablespoonful pineapple juice
few whole walnuts

METHOD

Slightly warm the treacle before measuring, to ensure an accurate measurement. Drain the can of pineapple and keep the juice. In a basin cream together the butter, sugar and treacle until light in colour and fluffy. Gradually beat in the lightly beaten egg. Fold in the sieved flour, pineapple, walnuts and 4 tablespoonsful of the pineapple juice. When evenly blended divide the mixture in half and put in 2 greased and lined 1-lb loaf tins, levelling off the top. Bake at approximately 325°F (170°C) or Mark 3 for 1–1¼ hours. When firm to the touch and evenly browned turn out and cool on a wire tray.

TO MAKE THE ICING Sieve the icing sugar into a small basin, and mix with the pineapple juice. When evenly blended spread over the top of the loaves and decorate with the whole walnuts.

SPICED FRUIT LOAVES

Ingredients

10 oz self-raising flour
1 level teaspoonful cinnamon
pinch salt
pinch ground cloves
pinch ground ginger
2 oz candied peel
2 oz sultanas
4 oz caster sugar
4 oz black treacle
generous ¼ pint milk

METHOD

Into a basin sieve the flour, cinnamon, salt, cloves and ginger. Add peel, sultanas and sugar, and stir together. Warm the treacle in the milk and mix together with the dry ingredients until smooth. Turn the mixture into 2 well greased 1-lb loaf tins and bake at approximately 325°F (170°C) or Mark 3 for 1–1¼ hours.

Turn out on to a cooling tray while still warm, and allow to cool.

Serve sliced with butter, or alternatively ice the top with glacé icing and decorate with slices of crystallized ginger.

SPICED HONEY LOAF

Ingredients

2 oz butter
5 oz liquid honey
5 oz Demerara sugar
10 oz plain flour
pinch salt
1 level teaspoonful bicarbonate of soda
1 level teaspoonful baking powder
1 level teaspoonful mixed spice
1 level teaspoonful ground ginger
1 level teaspoonful cinnamon
3 oz candied peel
1 egg (size 3)
¼ pint milk
few flaked almonds for top

METHOD

Put the butter into a pan over a low heat until just melted. Draw the pan from the heat and stir in the honey and sugar. Cool. Sift the flour, salt, raising agents and spices into a mixing bowl and add the peel.

Beat the egg in the milk and mix into the dry ingredients together with the cooled honey mixture. Beat until smooth then pour into a greased and lined 2-lb loaf tin. Scatter the almonds over the top and bake at approximately 350°F (180°C) or Mark 4 until firm, for about 1–1¼ hours.

Serve sliced and buttered, or as a spicy bread.

BREAD & SCONES

More and more people, I'm happy to see, are making their own bread for a variety of reasons, be it bakery strikes, the cost of a loaf or simply that they get real satisfaction in making and eating it.

There are recipes for white and brown bread using fresh or dried yeast. Both of these doughs need only one rising, when the dough is in the tin. I have also included some scone loaves which are made without yeast, but can be eaten instead of bread.

Since pizzas are so popular I have included a basic recipe with a wide selection of fillings. Then there's Fancy Bread, Tea Cakes and Mother's Fruit Scones which always turn out well and she gets many requests from my friends to make a batch when they're calling.

BASIC DOUGH

Ingredients	**YEAST LIQUID**
	¼ oz fresh yeast
	¼ pint warm water
	OR
	¼ teaspoonful sugar
	¼ pint warm water
	1 teaspoonful dried yeast
Other ingredients	**8 oz plain white flour OR**
	white and brown mixed
	1 teaspoonful salt
	¼ oz lard

METHOD

For fresh yeast, blend the yeast in the warm water.

If using dried yeast – dissolve the sugar in the water and sprinkle on the dried yeast. Leave until frothy – about 10 minutes.

Mix the dry ingredients and rub in the lard. Add the yeast liquid and work to a firm dough that leaves the bowl clean.

Turn the dough out on to a lightly-floured board and knead until smooth and elastic.

Put the dough to rise inside a large polythene bag until it doubles in size.

BROWN BREAD

Ingredients **3 lb wholemeal flour**
**2 oz fresh yeast or 2 rounded teaspoonsful of
dried yeast**
1 level tablespoonful brown sugar or treacle
4 level teaspoonsful salt
2 pints (approx.) warm milk and water

METHOD
Sieve half the flour into a warm basin. Mix milk and water, sugar or
treacle and yeast in a jug and stir well.

Make a batter with the flour in the basin and beat well. Cover the basin
and put in a warm place until it froths, approximately 10–15 minutes.

Add sufficient of the remaining flour and all the salt to make a soft,
scone-like dough. Knead the dough well for 5–10 minutes.

Divide dough in half, flatten each piece and then roll up to fit two
greased 2-lb loaf tins. Put the dough into the tins, put these into a polythene bag to rise to the tops of the tins. Brush lightly with a little milk and
bake at approximately 450°F (230°C) or Mark 8 for 30–40 minutes.

To test when the loaves are cooked, turn them out of the tins, rap the
bottom of each loaf with the knuckles and if they sound hollow they are
done. Cool on a wire rack.

CHEESE SCONE RING

Ingredients **8 oz self-raising flour**
pinch salt
pinch cayenne pepper
2 oz butter
3 oz Cheddar cheese (grated)
1 oz Parmesan cheese (grated)
approx. ¼ pint milk

METHOD
In a basin sieve the flour and seasonings, rub in the butter until it resembles
fine breadcrumbs. Stir in the cheese and add sufficient milk to make a soft
dough.

Turn out on to a floured board and knead lightly. Roll out ½ in. thick,
cut into rounds with a 1½-in. – 2-in. cutter.

Place in a circle on a greased baking tin, making sure the scones just touch each other. Bake at approximately 450°F (230°C) or Mark 8 for 8–10 minutes.

Serve in a ring on a serving plate and place a glass with celery in the centre.

N.B. When they are a day old, they are delicious toasted.

(approximately 10 scones)

COUNTRY STYLE PIZZA

Ingredients   **basic dough already risen**
oil for brushing
FILLING
1 lb tomatoes, sliced or large can (drained)
1 small onion (sliced)
salt and pepper
1 teaspoonful thyme, oregano or rosemary
12 oz Cheddar cheese (grated)
4 rashers streaky bacon (cut in strips)
6 pickled prunes (halved)

METHOD
Roll the risen dough to fit a greased baking tin 13 in. by 9 in. Brush the dough with a little oil, cover with tomatoes and onion and season well.

Sprinkle on the cheese and form a lattice with the bacon strips. Decorate with pickled prunes.

Bake at approximately 450°F (230°C) or Mark 8 for 25–35 minutes until the cheese is bubbling and browned.

ALTERNATIVE FILLINGS FOR PIZZA

PIZZA FRANCESCANA
4 oz Bel Paese cheese (thinly sliced)
4 oz mushrooms (sliced)
8 oz ham (cut in strips)
8 oz tomatoes (sliced)
salt and pepper
Place cheese on rolled out dough, cover with mushrooms, ham and finally tomatoes. Season well. Bake as already directed.

PIZZA SAN REMO
1 lb onions (sliced)
2 oz butter
1 can sardines in oil
9–12 black olives (stoned)

Sauté the onions in the butter until they become transparent – about 6 minutes. Place on the dough and season well. Arrange sardines and olives on top. Bake as already directed.

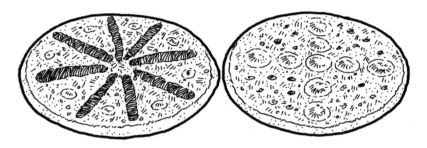

COUNTRY STYLE SAUSAGE ROLLS

Ingredients **basic dough**
FILLING
4 oz Cheddar cheese (grated)
1 lb sausage meat
little mustard

METHOD
Roll out the risen dough into a rectangle 12 in. by 9 in. Cut the dough in half lengthwise.

Roll the sausage meat into 2 rolls 12 in. long and place one on each piece of dough.

Cover the meat with $3\frac{1}{2}$ oz of cheese and dot with mustard. Roll the dough up like a swiss roll, wetting the edges to seal them. Brush with milk and cut into required lenths, i.e. 2 to 3 in.

Place the remaining cheese on top and place on greased baking tins.

Slash the tops to allow the steam to escape during baking. Bake at approximately 450°F (230°C) or Mark 8 for 15–20 minutes.
N.B. For extra-light rolls, after slashing the tops place the tins in a polythene bag and leave to rise until light and puffy – about 20 to 30 minutes, then cook as mentioned above. (14–16 rolls)

DROPPED SCONES

Ingredients

8 oz self-raising flour
pinch salt
2 oz caster sugar
2 eggs (beaten)
good ¼ pint of milk
little fat to grease frying pan

LEMON BUTTER
2 oz butter
grated rind 1 lemon
2 teaspoonsful lemon juice
2 level teaspoonfuls caster sugar

METHOD

Sieve the flour and salt into a basin and add the sugar. Make a well in the centre of the mixture, pour in the eggs and milk slowly, beating all the time, to ensure a smooth batter.

Allow the mixture to stand for 10–15 minutes. Lightly grease the frying pan and heat to a moderate temperature. Drop dessertspoonsful of the mixture into the pan, cook until the top bubbles and the underside is brown, then turn over and brown the other side. Cool in a clean folded tea towel.

TO MAKE LEMON BUTTER Beat the butter until soft then blend in the other ingredients.   (approx. 20 scones)

ENRICHED WHITE DOUGH

Ingredients

YEAST LIQUID
1 oz fresh yeast
8 fluid oz warm milk
1 (25g) tablet of ascorbic acid

Other Ingredients

1 lb plain white flour
1 level teaspoonful sugar
1 level teaspoonful salt
2 oz margarine
1 egg (beaten)
little milk to glaze

Prepare the yeast liquid by blending the yeast with the milk and adding the crushed ascorbic acid tablet, stir until dissolved.

Sieve flour and salt together, add sugar and rub in margarine until it resembles fine breadcrumbs.

Mix in yeast liquid and egg with a wooden spoon and work to a firm dough, adding a little extra flour if necessary until the sides of the bowl are clean.

Turn dough out on to a lightly floured board and knead well for up to 10 minutes. Continue until the dough feels elastic and firm and no longer sticky.

Flatten dough slightly then roll up like a swiss roll, tuck the ends in and place in a 2-lb loaf tin which has been greased.

Place tin in a polythene bag and leave to rise to just above the top of the tin.

Brush top with a little milk, taking care not to spoil the shape, and bake at approximately 375°F (190°C) or Mark 5 for about 40–45 minutes.

The loaf is cooked when it is removed from the tin, turned upside down and the base tapped with the knuckles – if it sounds hollow it's ready. Cool on a wire cooling tray.

N.B. This amount of dough will also make:

two cottage loaves or two cob loaves or two plaits, or one dozen rolls.

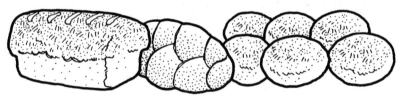

ICED ALMOND FRUIT PLAIT

Ingredients ½ **quantity of enriched white dough**
2 oz currants
2 oz sultanas
½ oz mixed peel
1 oz almonds (chopped)
grated rind ½ lemon
ICING
4 oz icing sugar
approx. 1 tablespoonful lemon juice
1 oz flaked almonds (toasted)

METHOD

Mix the fruit, peel, almonds and lemon rind into the dough until evenly mixed.

Divide the dough in half and roll each piece into a roll 12 in. to 14 in. long.

Arrange the rolls in a cross on the table, then taking the two ends of the bottom roll cross them over the centre of the top roll, laying each end down on the opposite side. Repeat this with the other roll, building up the plait vertically.

Cross each roll alternately until all the dough is used up. Finally gather the short ends together and lay the plait down on its side.

Place the plait on a large lightly oiled baking tin, brush with a little milk and place in a polythene bag until it doubles in size. Bake at approximately 375°F (190°C) or Mark 5 for about 30 minutes.

It is cooked when it sounds hollow, then cool on a wire cooling tray until cold.

TO ICE Blend the icing sugar with sufficient lemon juice to give a pouring consistency. Spoon over the top of the plait, allowing it to run down the sides. Sprinkle the almonds on top.

MOTHER'S FRUIT SCONES

Ingredients

8 oz self-raising flour
1 level teaspoonful cream of tartar
½ level teaspoonful bicarbonate of soda
2 oz butter
2 oz sultanas or mixed fruit
2 oz granulated sugar
approx. ¼ pint milk

METHOD

Lightly grease two baking tins.

In a basin sieve the flour, cream of tartar and bicarbonate of soda. Rub the butter into the flour until it resembles fine breadcrumbs, add the fruit and sugar and mix to a soft, but not sticky, dough with the milk. Roll out on a lightly floured board to ½ in. thickness, cut into rounds with a 2½-in cutter. Place on tins and bake at approximately 425°F (220°C) or Mark 7 for about 12 minutes.

When cold store in an airtight container. (Approx. 12 scones)

NELLIE'S TEA CAKES

Ingredients

1 lb self-raising flour
1 oz lard
4 oz mixed dried fruit
½ oz chopped candied peel
1½ oz caster sugar
1 oz compressed yeast
pinch salt
approx. ⅓ pint warm milk to mix

METHOD

Sieve the flour into a basin and rub in the lard. Add fruit, peel and salt. Mix the yeast and sugar together until the yeast becomes liquid. Add one-third of a pint of warm milk to the yeast mixture, stir together and pour into the dry ingredients. Mix all well together with a spoon or the hand until the mixture leaves the sides of the basin.

Cover with a piece of polythene or a cloth, and set in a warm place to rise, about 1½ hours or until the mixture has doubled its size. Turn the mixture out on to a floured board and knead well with the heel of the hand until the mixture is pliable and not sticky. Divide equally into 12 pieces, mould into round buns, place on warmed baking tins, cover and allow to rise to double their size, about ½ hour. Bake at approximately 400°F (200°C) or Mark 6 for 10–15 minutes. When baked the buns should be golden brown on top, and sound hollow when tapped with the fingers on the base. Serve spread with butter, or if a day or two old, toasted with butter.   (12 cakes)

SCONE MEAL LOAVES

Ingredients　　　　**1½ lb brown scone meal (from health shops)**
　　　　　　　　　　2 oz butter or margarine
　　　　　　　　　　½ teaspoonful salt
　　　　　　　　　　¼ pint milk
　　　　　　　　　　½ pint water

METHOD

Well grease two 6-in. – 7-in. sponge sandwich tins.

Put flour and salt into a basin and rub in the fat. When it has been rubbed in finely add all the liquid and mix well together.

Turn out on to a lightly floured board, divide in half and mould each piece into a round. Flatten the top slightly, put into the prepared tins and bake at approximately 425°F (220°C) or Mark 7 for 25–35 minutes, or until the crust turns golden brown.

WHITE SCONE LOAF

Ingredients　　　　**1 lb self-raising flour**
　　　　　　　　　　1 heaped teaspoonful salt
　　　　　　　　　　½ pint cold water

METHOD

Sieve the flour and salt into a basin, then mix to a pliable dough with the water.

Turn the dough out on to a lightly floured board and knead lightly until smooth.

Divide the mixture in half and shape into 6-in. rounds, then put on to greased baking tins.

Bake at approximately 450°F (230°C) or Mark 8 for about 20 minutes, when the top should be lightly brown and the base should sound hollow when tapped with the knuckles.

N.B. These loaves should be eaten freshly baked as they do not contain yeast.

PRESERVES

When I open my preserves cupboard on a cold winter's day I feel the effort of making them during the summer months was well worth while. How lovely it is to eat some of the fruits of summer in the depths of winter.

The first preserve I make each year is Marmalade. Blackberry and Apple Jam remind me of the glut of apples we had. Gooseberry Jelly, made with our own gooseberries and that big marrow in the garden that we made into Marrow and Ginger Jam. The young mint was made into Mint Jelly and the old stringy beetroots ended up as Chutney.

These and many other recipes are included, so why not make some, because they really are so useful during the long cold winter months.

APPLE AND DATE CHUTNEY

Ingredients

1 lb cooking apples (weight after peeling and coring)
1 lb stoned dates
½ lb onions
2 oz brown sugar
2 level tablespoonsful black treacle
1 pint vinegar
1 level teaspoonful ground ginger
1 level teaspoonful dry mustard
½ teaspoonful salt
pinch cayenne pepper

METHOD

Mince or finely chop the dates, apples and onions. Put these into a large saucepan together with all the other ingredients.

Simmer gently until they form a thick pulp, then fill heated jars to the brim, and cover with a layer of thick waxed vinegar-proof paper. Then either cover with a parchment covering or a non-metal lid. Label and store in a cool, dry place when cold.

N.B. This is very nice eaten with cold pork or meat pie, and can be made into a nice sandwich with cheddar cheese.

(yield approximately 4 lb)

BLACKBERRY AND APPLE JAM

Ingredients   **2 lb cooking apples**
                       ¾ pint water
                       2 lb blackberries
                       4 lb sugar

METHOD

Peel, core and slice the apples, then put them into a preserving pan with the water and simmer until tender. Add the blackberries and simmer until they are tender. Take the pan from the cooker, add the sugar and stir until it dissolves. Return the pan to the cooker, putting it on a high heat. Boil quickly for 10 minutes, stirring from time to time. Test for a set, and when you're satisfied that it's ready, remove the pan from the heat. Skim and allow to cool a little before putting into hot jars. This will ensure that the fruit does not rise in the jars. Then cover and seal.

(yield approximately 6 lb)

BLACKCURRANT JAM

Ingredients   **1 lb blackcurrants**
                       1¼ lb sugar

METHOD

Into a pan put the fruit and sugar and bring slowly to boiling point, stirring quite frequently to ensure the sugar dissolves. Once this happens boil really fast for 5 minutes. Remove the pan from the heat, test for a set and put in hot jars. Cover in the usual way.
N.B. Any soft fruits can be made into jam in the above way, and will keep for years.   (yield approximately 2 lb)

CHERRY JAM

Ingredients   **4 lb fresh cherries**
                       3½ lb preserving sugar
                       4 small lemons

METHOD

Stone about three dozen cherries, break the stones and remove the kernels.

Put the kernels into the pan with the lemon juice and cherries, and cook very slowly over a low heat to begin with. After about 15 minutes bring the ingredients to simmering point and continue cooking until the fruit is tender, by which time the liquid will also be somewhat reduced. Next add the sugar, stirring all the time, until the ingredients come to the boil, then continue boiling fairly briskly until setting point is reached, approximately 20–30 minutes. When ready put into hot jars and cover at once in the usual way.   (yield approximately 5 lb)

GINGER PEAR PRESERVE

Ingredients   **3 lb home grown pears**
4 oz finely chopped stem ginger
2½ lb granulated sugar

METHOD
Peel, core and cut the pears into small pieces. Put these into a basin in layers with the sugar, cover with a cloth and leave to stand overnight. The following day turn the mixture from the basin into a large saucepan or preserving pan, add the ginger and cook gently until the fruit is transparent and the syrup thickens. Once the fruit is transparent, which takes quite a long time, bring the preserve to the boil, and boil quickly for 5 minutes. Remove the pan from the heat, allow to cool slightly and then remove the scum from the top. Pot in the usual way and label.
                              (yield approximately 3 lb)

GOOSEBERRY CHEESE

Ingredients   **1 lb fresh young gooseberries**
1 small garlic clove
2 oz raw onion (finely chopped)
¾ gill water
1¼ gills malt vinegar
5 oz caster sugar
1 teaspoonful salt
¼ level teaspoonful cayenne pepper
3 level teaspoonsful mixed spice

Top, tail and wash the gooseberries, then cut in half and put into a saucepan with the onion, chopped garlic and water. Cook until soft. Add all other ingredients and simmer gently until the mixture begins to thicken, or if liked a little thicker, cook for a longer period. Pot in heated jars, cover, seal down and label. This is excellent with cold pork or duck.

(yield approximately 2 lb)

GOOSEBERRY JELLY

Ingredients   **5 lb gooseberries**
                 water
                 sugar

METHOD

Wash the gooseberries and put them into a large pan (there is no need to top and tail them). Simmer over a gentle heat with sufficient water just to cover the fruit. When the gooseberries are very soft, tip the contents of the pan into a jelly bag. Hang up and allow to drip, until no more juice is coming from the bag, but DO NOT SQUEEZE it or you will make the jelly cloudy.

Measure the juice out into pints and put into the pan, and allow $1\frac{1}{4}$ lb of sugar to each pint. Stir all well together, and once the sugar has dissolved, bring to the boil and continue boiling until setting point is reached. Pot and cover in the usual way.   (yield approximately 7 lb)

GOOSEBERRY AND STRAWBERRY JAM

Ingredients   **2 lb gooseberries**
                 4 lb strawberries
                 6 lb sugar

METHOD

Top and tail the gooseberries and cut in half with a pair of kitchen scissors. Put them into a preserving or saucepan, with sufficient water to just cover the fruit. Simmer until all the gooseberries are soft, then add the strawberries and sugar. Stir all well together and keep on a medium heat until the sugar has dissolved, stirring from time to time. Bring to the boil and keep boiling until setting point is reached (i.e. a little placed on a saucer will wrinkle when pushed with the finger). Allow the jam to cool slightly and remove any scum, before pouring into hot jars. Seal down as for other jams.   (yield approximately 4 lb)

LIME MARMALADE

Ingredients
3 lb limes
5 pints water
6½ lb sugar

METHOD
Squeeze the juice from the limes, and put the pips and pith into a muslin bag, tie securely.

Mince or slice the peel.

Put the peel, water and muslin bag into a preserving pan and cook the fruit until it is soft, which is when the peel begins to sink.

Remove the bag of pith and pips and when cold squeeze over the pan, add the sugar and, once it has dissolved, boil rapidly until setting point is reached. Pour into hot jars and seal down in the usual way. Store in a dry and airy storecupboard. (yield approximately 10 lb)

MARROW CREAM

Ingredients
3 lb peeled and deseeded marrow
3 lb preserving sugar
6 oz butter
1 oz crushed root ginger (tied in a muslin bag)
4 lemons (rind and juice)

METHOD
Steam the marrow until tender and then rub it through a nylon or hair sieve, to give about 1¾ pints of pulp. Put the pulp into a large saucepan or preserving pan and add all the other ingredients. Allow this to simmer until the consistency is like thick cream. Then pour into hot, clean jars and seal down with jam-pot covers, label and store in a dry cool place.

N.B. This cream will not set as do other jams, but it will keep a long time providing the instructions for making it are carried out. It is more like the consistency of lemon curd. (yield approximately 5½ lb)

MARROW GINGER JAM

Ingredients

1½ lb marrow (seeds and skin removed)
1½ lb granulated sugar
½ oz root ginger
1 lemon (grated rind and juice)

METHOD

Cut the marrow into small cubes about ¼ in. square and put them into a basin in layers, alternating with the sugar. Cover the basin with a clean cloth and leave in a cool place overnight or up to 24 hours.

Crush the ginger with a hammer and put into a small muslin bag. Put the marrow and sugar into a saucepan together with the ginger, lemon rind and lemon juice.

Bring very slowly to the boil and continue cooking until the marrow is transparent. Boil quicker at this stage until it starts to set, but do not expect it to set as firm as other jams.

The consistency when ready for potting should be a thick syrup. Cover and label in the usual way.   (yield approximately 2 lb)

MINT JELLY

Ingredients

6 lb bright green apples
sugar
water
bunch fresh mint (minced or finely chopped)
juice of 4 lemons
green vegetable colouring (optional)

METHOD

Wash and cut up the apples, put them into a pan with a few sprigs of mint, lemon juice and sufficient water to just cover the apples.

Simmer these ingredients to a soft pulp.

Strain the liquid off, and to each pint of liquid add 1 lb of sugar. Heat together until the sugar has dissolved.

Boil rapidly for 5 minutes, add the mint and colouring and continue boiling until setting point is reached. Skim, and pour into hot jars. Seal in the usual way.

MRS PARSON'S BEETROOT CHUTNEY

Ingredients

1 lb cooked beetroot
½ lb peeled and cored sour apples
¼ lb onions or shallots
¼ lb Demerara sugar
1 oz salt
½ oz mixed pickling spice
¾ pint malt vinegar

METHOD

Mince the beetroot, apples and onions. Put these into a large saucepan, add the sugar, salt, the pickling spice tied in a muslin bag and half the vinegar. Boil until well blended – about 30 minutes.

Add the remaining vinegar and boil again until the mixture is smooth and the consistency of jam – about 25 minutes. Pour the chutney into clean hot jars while still hot and cover in the usual way as for jam.

(yield approximately 2 lb)

ORTANIQUE AND LEMON MARMALADE

Ingredients

1 lb ortaniques
1 large or 2 small juicy lemons } **½ pint juice**
1 pint cold water
2 lb preserving or granulated sugar

METHOD

Wash the fruit and cut in half. Squeeze out all the juice and remove as much pith as possible from the shells. Put the skins through the mincer, and the pith and pips into a muslin bag, tying it securely. Into a saucepan put the peel, juice, water and muslin bag. Cook these ingredients slowly until the peel is soft when pressed between the finger and thumb. It will probably take 1–2 hours, during which time the water content will be reduced by approximately half.

When the peel is tender remove the muslin bag and, when cool, squeeze into the pan, add the sugar and dissolve gently over a gentle heat. When dissolved boil quickly until a set is obtained, i.e. when a little of the marmalade is put onto a saucer and has become quite cold, it should wrinkle when moved with the finger. Allow to cool slightly in the pan before pouring into hot jars. Cover and label.   (yield approximately 3 lb)

PLUM CHUTNEY

Ingredients

2 lb plums (stoned)
1 lb apples (chopped)
1 lb shallots (chopped)
1 lb raisins
6 oz brown sugar
1 teaspoonful ground ginger
1 teaspoonful allspice
pinch of: cayenne pepper, cloves, mustard
  and nutmeg
1 oz salt
1 pint vinegar

METHOD

Put all the ingredients together in a saucepan, and mix well. Bring to the boil and then simmer until the chutney is the thickness you like it. Pot in hot jars and seal. Store in a cool, dry place.   (Approx. $4\frac{1}{2}$ lb)

RED CURRANT JELLY

Ingredients

6 lb redcurrants (just ripe)
$1\frac{1}{2}$ pints water
sugar

METHOD

Wash the fruit thoroughly, removing any leaves, but not the stalks. Put the fruit into a preserving pan with the water and simmer very gently over a low heat until the fruit is cooked and the berries pulped. Pour the contents of the pan into a jelly bag, tie securely and allow to drip for several hours, or over-night.

Weigh the extract which has dripped from the bag and put it into the preserving pan, bring to the boil and boil for 5 minutes. Then add an equal weight of sugar and stir until the sugar has all dissolved. Bring to the boil again and boil briskly for 5–10 minutes, stirring occasionally. Put a little jelly on a plate and test for a set (i.e. when cold if pushed with the finger the jelly should wrinkle). Finally skim if necessary, pour into hot jars and cover at once. Once you've labelled it, put it into a cool, dry place. This will keep it in good condition for use during the following months.   (yield approximately 6 lb)

RICH DARK MARMALADE

Ingredients
2 lb Seville oranges
1 large lemon
7 pints cold water
6 lb Demerara sugar
3 oz West Indian black treacle

METHOD

Wash and dry the fruit, cut in half and squeeze out all the juice. Tie the pith and pips loosely in a muslin bag. Slice the skins into medium thick shreds. Into a preserving pan put the juice, muslin bag, peel and water and simmer until the peel is tender, about 1½ hours, and the liquid has reduced by half.

Remove the bag of pips and pith, let it cool slightly and then squeeze out any juice, very gently into the pan. Remove the pan from the heat, add the sugar and treacle and return to the heat, simmering only until the sugar has dissolved. Boil rapidly until setting point is reached – approximately 30 minutes. Test by your usual method, pour into clean jars and cover down firmly. (yield approximately 9¼ lb)

SEVILLE ORANGE JELLY

Ingredients
5 Seville oranges
1 lemon **1¼ lb in weight**
3 pints water
granulated or preserving sugar

METHOD

Wash the fruit and cut each orange and the lemon into eight sections. Soak the fruit in the water overnight.

Next day – put the fruit and water into the preserving pan and simmer until the fruit is very soft, approximately 2 hours.

Strain the contents of the preserving pan through a jelly bag and allow to drain overnight. (On no account squeeze the bag, or the jelly will become cloudy.)

Allow 1 lb of sugar to each pint of juice, then heat the juice and add the sugar, stirring until dissolved. Boil rapidly until setting point is reached. Remove any scum from the top of the jelly, cool slightly, and pour into warmed jars. Cover with jam pot covers and label.

(yield approximately 3 lb)

STRAWBERRY JAM

Ingredients   **2½ lb strawberries**
       3 lb 2 oz preserving sugar
       3 tablespoonsful fresh lemon juice

METHOD

Put the strawberries and sugar together in a heavy based saucepan, or preserving pan, over a low heat.

Give an occasional stir until the fruit and sugar are well mixed. Continue cooking over a low heat until the fruit is soft and the sugar dissolved; then raise the heat; add the lemon juice and boil fast, about 10–15 minutes, or until it sets when tested.

Bottle in clean hot jars and tie down as for other jams.

(yield approximately 4 lb)

RECIPES FOR VEGETARIANS

I have included this section on vegetarian dishes as a result of the many letters I have received over the years. To ensure the recipes are correct the Food and Cookery sections of the Vegetarian Society have supplied and tested all these dishes, especially for this book.

As you will see, there is a fairly wide range including soups, salads, savoury dishes, desserts and cakes. I'm not a vegetarian but I have tried a number of vegetarian meals and find them interesting and extremely tasty. So why don't you have a meatless day from time to time and enjoy a change of diet.

All the ingredients are readily available from your local shops or from health food stores.

AUBERGINE PATE

Ingredients
**2 medium sized aubergines
oil for frying
1 small clove garlic
juice 1 small lemon
pepper and salt or celery salt**

METHOD
Peel and slice aubergines fairly thinly. Put plenty of vegetable oil in a frying pan and when it is hot, add the aubergine, just enough to cover the bottom of the pan.

Turn the slices as they are cooking and let them fry gently until soft and lightly browned. Add extra oil if necessary.

Put the cooked slices as they are ready into an electric blender and when they are all done add the garlic, strained lemon juice and plenty of seasoning.

Blend first on a low speed and then on a high speed until the mixture is quite smooth. It should be fairly soft, so add a little extra oil if necessary, while it is blending.

Put in a serving dish and chill until required.

Serve on hot toast or crispbread with a green salad.   (6 portions)

BEAN AND RICE PLATTER

Ingredients

8 oz black-eyed beans
1 bay leaf
½ teaspoonful salt
1 teaspoonful marjoram
4 oz whole grain rice
1 teaspoonful salt
sprigs mint

METHOD

Remove any foreign matter from the beans, wash in cold water and leave to soak in fresh cold water for about 30 minutes.

Cook slowly, with bay leaf, until tender (about 40 minutes) adding salt and marjoram after 30 minutes.

Meanwhile, cook the rice in salted water, it will take about the same time as the beans.

Arrange alternate strips of rice and beans across the width of a hot flat dish. Stick sprigs of mint between the rows as a garnish. Serve hot with tomato sauce.

Alternately, as a cold accompaniment to salad.

When the beans are cool, stir in half a cupful of French dressing. Arrange on the dish while rice is still warm and garnish with small tomatoes as follows: Cut the tomatoes into 7 or 8 sections with a sharp knife, leaving the base uncut. Gently pull the tops apart and fill with some of the rice. Place a slice of stuffed olive on top of each.

N.B. Other kinds of beans can be used but they take longer to soak and cook.

(6 portions)

CHESTNUT STEW

Ingredients

1 lb chestnuts
¼ lb wholegrain rice
¼ lb mushrooms
1 Spanish onion
4 tomatoes
2 tablespoonsful vegetable oil
seasoning

Cook and peel chestnuts. Boil rice for 30–40 minutes.

Fry mushrooms, onion and two of the tomatoes in the oil then add chestnuts.

Surround chestnut stew with rice on a flat dish and garnish with remaining tomatoes which have been fried. (6 portions)

FRUITARIAN CAKE (Uncooked)

Ingredients **6 oz dates (chopped)**
6 oz raisins or sultanas
2 oz milled nuts (preferably cashews)
lemon juice
chopped nuts for decoration
extra $\frac{1}{2}$ oz milled nuts

METHOD
Pound or mince all ingredients together, using sufficient lemon juice to flavour, without making the mixture too sticky. Form into a cake shape.

Roll in a little milled nut and put a few chopped or whole nuts on top. It is best to chill in the refrigerator for a day or so before cutting.

This is quite different from the usual cake, being very concentrated and rather sticky. If made into small balls or little flat cakes, sandwich between rice paper. It is useful for packed lunches. (6″ × 6″)

FRUIT JELLY

Jellies for vegetarians must not contain gelatine which is frequently used in purchased jelly powders although there are certain ones in health food stores made with agar-agar. Agar-agar is extracted from certain seaweeds and is excellent for home use. 1 teaspoonful of powdered agar-agar will gel: 1 pint of fruit juice if used as below.

Ingredients **1 pint fruit juice (any kind)**
1 teaspoonful agar-agar

METHOD
Bring the juice to the boil then sprinkle in the powdered agar-agar and whisk or stir for two to three minutes until it is dissolved. Add any

sweetening required after the agar is dissolved and pour at once into a wetted mould or individual serving dishes.

The juice from stewed fruit can be gelled and then poured back over the fruit and when set the top of the sweet can be decorated with piped cream or nut cream.

N.B. A cold nut savoury (see 'Nutmeat' recipe) can be brushed over with a hot solution of yeast extract in water with agar dissolved in it. This makes a shiny finish. For this use 1 teaspoonful of agar-agar to $\frac{1}{2}$ pint water. (6 portions)

HONEYDEW RINGS

Ingredients   **1 large honeydew melon**
                     lettuce
                     2 cups fresh banana rings
                     French dressing
                     2 cups raspberries
                     2 cups seeded or seedless grapes
                     sprigs of mint

METHOD

Peel melon and cut into thick rings, removing seeds.

Put rings on the lettuce. Drop the banana rings into the dressing as soon as they are cut to prevent discolouration.

Fill the melon rings with raspberries, grapes and bananas and garnish with sprigs of mint. (4 portions)

LENTIL CURRY

Ingredients   **1 onion (chopped)**
                     1 clove garlic (crushed)
                     1 dessertspoonful curry powder
                     2 tablespoonsful vegetable oil
                     8 oz red lentils
                     1 pint water or vegetable stock
                     1 bay leaf
                     1 tablespoonful tomato purée
                     salt to taste

OPTIONAL ADDITIONS
dessicated coconut
chilli powder
soaked dried fruit

METHOD
Cook onion, garlic and curry powder with the oil and 1 tablespoonful of water for a few minutes.

Cook lentils in water or stock for about 10 minutes, then add curry mixture, bay leaf, tomato purée and salt. Continue cooking gently until the lentils are tender. There should be little or no liquid when they are done.

Serve at once with hot rice.

N.B. Besides being traditional and a pleasant combination, lentils and rice eaten together supply excellent protein.   (6 portions)

MUSHROOM SOUP

Ingredients   **2 oz onion (sliced)**
2 tablespoonsful vegetable oil
1 tablespoonful 100 per cent wholemeal flour
2 pints vegetable stock
8 oz mushrooms (finely chopped)
seasoning
chopped parsley, chervil or chives

METHOD
Cook the onions in the oil for a few minutes, shaking so that they do not stick together.

Stir in the flour, add the stock and mushrooms

Simmer for 30 minutes, add seasoning to taste and sprinkle chopped herbs on top when serving.   (4 portions)

NETTLE SOUP

Ingredients
**3 oz young nettle leaves
1 small onion (chopped)
1 tablespoonful vegetable oil
¼ lb potatoes (peeled and diced)
2 pints vegetable stock
1 teaspoonful yeast extract (dissolved in stock)
1 teaspoonful marjoram or sage
2 tablespoonsful cream or nut cream**

METHOD

Use tender tops of the nettles, wash and remove the stalks.

Cook like spinach without adding any extra water, on a low heat. When tender, chop well.

Sauté onion in the oil until pale golden, add potatoes and continue cooking, gradually adding the vegetable stock.

When potatoes are soft, add nettles and herbs. Either cook for a further 15 minutes or liquidize, re-heat and serve at once with a little cream on top.   (6 portions)

NUTMEAT

Ingredients
**1 large onion
1 oz vegetable oil
3 oz cashew nuts (milled)
3 oz hazel or walnuts (milled)
3 oz wholemeal breadcrumbs
2 oz rolled oats
1 oz wholemeal flour
1 teaspoonful yeast extract
seasoning
1 teaspoonful mixed herbs**

Chop the onion and cook in the oil. Mix nuts, breadcrumbs, oats and flour.

Dissolve yeast extract and seasoning in a teacupful of hot water, add herbs and combine all ingredients, adding a little more water if necessary to bind.

Form into a nice shape, dot with nut fat or vegetable margarine and bake for 40 minutes at 400°F (200°C) or Mark 6.

Alternatively steam ingredients in a pudding basin for 1½ hours, *or* form into rissoles, coat them with crumbs and fry in hot oil, *or* use to make pasties, sausage rolls etc. (4 portions)

OAT AND VEGETABLE SOUP

Ingredients

2 Spanish onions
2 small turnips
1½ cups rolled oats
1 pint boiling water
1 pint milk or plant milk
pepper and salt to taste

METHOD

Cut up the vegetables into small pieces and put them with the rolled oats into the boiling water. Cook until tender, then either sieve or liquidize in a blender.

Add the milk, season and re-heat.

Serve with either chopped parsley or grated cheese with a pinch of nutmeg. (6 portions)

ORIGINAL FRUIT MUESLI

Ingredients

1 level tablespoonful rolled oats
   or preferably medium oatmeal
1 tablespoonful lemon juice
1 tablespoonful plant milk or nut milk
1 large apple (about 7 oz in weight)
1 tablespoonful nuts (milled)
sugar or honey if desired

METHOD

Soak oatmeal in 3 tablespoonsful of cold water overnight.

In the morning add lemon juice, milk and any sweetening.

Wash apple but do not peel, grate quickly into the oatmeal mixture, stirring to blend Serve at once with milled nuts sprinkled on top.

N.B. The nicest mueslis also include a little soaked dried fruit such as chopped dates or raisins. In this case no other sweetening should be necessary. Any other fruit may be used and soft fruits, such as blackcurrants, (mashed but not cooked) could take the place of the apple.

A mixture of whole uncooked cereals can take the place of oatmeal alone, but oatmeal is recommended for beginners. The quantity of cereal should never exceed 1 tablespoonful per person and must always be soaked. ⠀⠀⠀⠀⠀⠀⠀⠀⠀⠀⠀⠀⠀⠀⠀⠀⠀⠀⠀⠀⠀⠀⠀⠀⠀⠀-⠀⠀(4 portions)

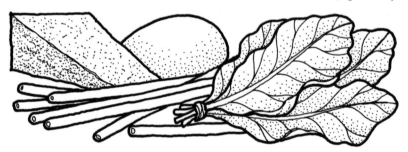

PASTA FLORENTINE

Ingredients

8 oz whole wheat long macaroni
1 lb spinach or nettles
4 eggs
4 oz cheese
seasoning to taste

METHOD

Cook the long macaroni in boiling water for 10–12 minutes and meanwhile cook spinach or nettles separately.

Drain macaroni and put in the centre of a hot greased dish, arranging spinach round it.

Make a well in the centre of the macaroni and fill it with the eggs and grated cheese which have been beaten well together.

Cook for 10 minutes at 400°F (200°C) or Mark 6.

If a strip of foil is placed over the spinach it will keep it moist whilst the dish is in the oven. ⠀⠀⠀⠀⠀⠀⠀⠀⠀⠀⠀⠀⠀⠀⠀⠀⠀⠀⠀⠀⠀⠀⠀⠀(4 portions)

PINEAPPLE/COCONUT SALAD

Ingredients

1 cup pineapple (cubed)
1 cup coconut (grated)
2 cups cabbage (finely shredded)
mayonnaise
lettuce
radishes

METHOD

Combine the pineapple, coconut and cabbage with the mayonnaise. Serve on a bed of lettuce, garnished with the radishes.

To get the best effect, the radishes should have been cut radially several times from the top downwards and left to soak in cold water for a short while. They will then have the appearance of small flowers.   (4 portions)

SESAME FLAPJACKS

Ingredients

4 oz vegetarian margarine
2 tablespoonsful dark syrup
8 oz rolled oats
2 oz sesame seeds
2 oz Muscavado sugar
¼ teaspoonful salt

METHOD

Melt margarine and syrup and stir into other ingredients, leaving a few sesame seeds to press into the top.

Press into a shallow greased tin and bake 25 minutes at 400°F (200°C) or Mark 6. Mark into squares while still warm and remove from tin when cold. Store in an airtight container.   (12 pieces)

SPAGHETTI BOLOGNESE

Ingredients

2 onions (chopped)
1 tablespoonful vegetable oil
2 × 14 oz cans tomatoes
4 oz textured vegetable protein (mince style)
12 oz whole wheat spaghetti
1 tablespoonful cornflour
1 tablespoonful water

METHOD

Fry onions in the oil, drain tomatoes and mix with onions and tomato purée.

Add the textured protein (previously soaked in hot vegetable stock). Simmer gently for 15 minutes.

Meanwhile cook the spaghetti in boiling salted water for 12 minutes. If the sauce needs thickening, blend cornflour and water add it to the pan and stir on the hotplate.

Put spaghetti on a hot dish and surround it with the sauce.

N.B. Textured vegetable protein, if unflavoured, should always be soaked in a strongly flavoured stock for 10–20 minutes at least. Use a stock cube which is guaranteed vegetarian or salted vegetable water in which a large teaspoonful of yeast extract has been dissolved. (4–6 portions)

SPICED ARTICHOKES

(with textured vegetable protein)

Ingredients
$\frac{1}{2}$ teaspoonful salt
$\frac{1}{4}$ teaspoonful chilli powder
1 bay leaf
$\frac{1}{2}$ teaspoonful powdered cumin
$\frac{1}{2}$ teaspoonful oregano
1 clove garlic
4 oz onion (finely chopped)
4 oz textured vegetable protein (mince style)
1 lb Jerusalem artichokes
4 fl oz oil
1 tablespoonful wholemeal flour
1 oz tomato purée
1 teaspoonful yeast extract (optional)

METHOD

Mix salt, spices and crushed garlic, add 1 pint of boiling water and the textured protein. Leave to stand 20 minutes.

Meanwhile scrub, trim and cook artichokes in the minimum of water. Drain stock from the protein and keep in reserve.

Sweat protein in the oil, then blend in the flour and tomato purée, add the artichokes and simmer 10 minutes, adding more stock as required.

If yeast extract is used it is dissolved in the hot water when making the stock. (4 portions)

STUFFED ONIONS

Ingredients   **4 large Spanish onions**
1 small tomato
3 tablespoonsful wholemeal breadcrumbs
2 tablespoonsful walnuts (ground)
1–2 tablespoonsful vegetable oil
1 teaspoonful sage
seasoning

METHOD
Peel onions and steam whole until fairly soft.

Cool and scoop out the centres. Chop these with the tomato and blend all ingredients together. Stuff this mixture firmly into the onions, place them in a greased baking dish, arranging any excess stuffing around the onions. Bake in a moderate oven for 30 minutes at approximately 375°F (190°C) or Mark 5.   (4 portions)

SUMMER CASSEROLE

Ingredients   **1 tablespoonful vegetable oil**
2 lb fresh shelled peas
½ lb carrots
½ lb French beans (cut)
1 lb small new potatoes (well scrubbed)
2 heaped tablespoonsful vegetarian soup
  powder
sprig mint or 2 teaspoonsful dried mint

METHOD
Put oil in a casserole, then the vegetables with the potatoes on top. Cover with boiling water and cook slowly with the lid on for 45 minutes.

Mix soup powder with a little cold water, add liquid from the vegetables, then return to the casserole and bring back to boiling point.

Serve with a topping of freshly chopped parsley, this adds Vitamin C.
N.B. If you have no vegetarian soup powder, use 1 tablespoonful of plain flour and 1 tablespoonful of soya flour with yeast extract and seasoning. Tomato purée could also be added.   (4 portions)

SWEETCORN SOUP

Ingredients
1 large onion
1 pint boiling water
1 pint milk or plant milk
1 oz butter or vegetable oil
seasoning to taste
1 small can sweet corn

METHOD
Slice the onion and put into a saucepan with all other ingredients except the sweet corn. Cook for 10–15 minutes, add the corn and seasoning and cook a further 10 minutes. Serve very hot. (6 portions)

TOMATO AND RICE SAVOURY

Ingredients
1 onion
1 tablespoonful vegetable oil
3 medium tomatoes
8 oz cooked brown rice
4 oz cheese (grated)
1 teaspoonful marjoram or basil
seasoning

METHOD
Chop the onion and cook in oil until soft, add chopped tomatoes and cook a further 3 minutes.

Add all remaining ingredients.

This can be served cold on salad or put in the oven just long enough to heat through. (4 portions)

UNCOOKED NUT SAVOURIES

Ingredients
1 cupful cashew nuts (milled)
1 cupful hazel or walnuts (milled)
2 teaspoonsful onion (grated)
1 teaspoonful mint or basil (chopped)
salt and/or yeast extract to taste

METHOD

Mix and pound together all the ingredients with a very little water. Form into balls or small squares and serve with salad.

This recipe can have many variations, different nuts and herbs can be used, rolled oats or crushed shredded wheat added or chopped tomato, tomato purée, etc. If no cereal is used it is recommended that milled cashew be included as these help the mixture to bind.

The mixture can also be put into greased moulds, turned out and sliced.   (4–6 portions)

VEGETABLE PIES

Ingredients

PASTRY
9 oz 100 per cent wholemeal flour
½ teaspoonful salt
3 oz brazil nuts (ground)
4 oz vegetarian margarine
cold water
FILLING
4 oz onions
8 oz carrots
8 oz peas
1 oz plain flour
1 oz vegetable oil
1 small teaspoonful yeast extract
seasoning

METHOD

Mix flour, salt and brazil nuts together, lightly rub in margarine and bind together with cold water.

Chop onions, dice carrots and cook peas 5–10 minutes, using only enough water to cover the bottom of the pan.

When vegetables are cooked, drain off any excess liquid and make up to ¼ pint with additonal water. Thicken this liquid with the flour blended to a cream with a little cold water and the oil beaten in.

Bring to the boil and add the yeast extract and seasoning.

Roll out pastry and line some small, deep baking tins or foil dishes. Fill with the vegetables, combined with the thick sauce and cover with a pastry lid. Decorate edges, pierce a hole in the middle of each and glaze with beaten egg and milk. Bake 20 minutes at 400°F (200°C) or Mark 6.

RECIPES FOR DIABETICS

Once again this section of the book is included at your request and as these recipes have to be very carefully balanced in calories and carbohydrates, I contacted the British Diabetic Association.

They have tested and supplied all these recipes especially for this book and I know they will be of special interest to the people who are diabetic. On the other hand, I always like to try something new and I can assure you that the recipes in this section are fun to make and delicious to eat.

You will find a wide and interesting range including fish, cheese and savouries, tarts and cakes, biscuits and desserts. So why not make some for the family, I'm sure they will enjoy them.

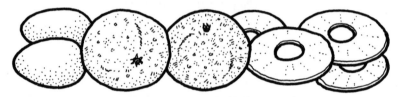

APPLE AND CINNAMON SLICE

6 slices – (each slice 5g carbohydrate 100 cals)

Ingredients
3 eggs
2 medium-sized cooking apples
crushed saccharin to taste (3 tablets)
8 oz cottage cheese
3 teaspoonsful cinnamon

METHOD

Preheat oven to 350°F (180°C) or Mark 4.

Separate the eggs and beat the yolks until creamy.

Core, peel and slice the apples very thinly and add the saccharin to taste.

Mix the yolks, apples, cottage cheese and cinnamon all well together until blended.

Beat the egg whites until stiff and fold into the mixture.

Line a 6-in. cake tin with lightly oiled greaseproof paper or foil.

Fill with the mixture and bake for about 30 minutes.

Sprinkle with a little extra cinnamon before serving.

BLACKBERRY AND APPLE CRUMBLE

2 servings – (each serving 20 carbohydrate 205 cals)

Ingredients
    4 oz cooking apples (peeled and cored)
    4 oz blackberries (fresh or frozen)
    saccharin (1 or 2 tablets)
    $\frac{1}{2}$ oz margarine
    $1\frac{1}{2}$ oz flour
    $\frac{1}{2}$ oz sorbitol

METHOD

Preheat the oven to 375°F (190°C) or Mark 5.

Slice the apples and stew with the blackberries, in just enough water to prevent them sticking to the pan (about $\frac{1}{2}$ cup).

When they are just soft but not mushy, remove the pan from the heat and stir in the crushed saccharin to taste.

Put the fruit into a small heatproof dish.

Rub the margarine into the flour until it is like fine breadcrumbs. Mix in the sorbitol.

Sprinkle the crumble evenly over the fruit and bake for 20–25 minutes.

CHEESE AND CHICKEN PANCAKES

4 servings – (each pancake 5g carbohydrate 200 cals)

Ingredients
    4 oz cooked chicken
    2 oz onion (1 small)
    chopped parsley
    $\frac{1}{4}$ oz butter
    seasoning
    2 eggs
    2 oz flour
    4 fl oz water
    oil for frying
    2 oz Cheddar cheese (grated)

METHOD

Mix chicken and onion and mix with parsley.

Melt butter in a pan, add chicken mixture and fry until onion is transparent. Add seasoning.

Make batter by mixing eggs, flour and water and season to taste. Leave to stand for 1 hour.

Heat oil in omelette pan and make 8 pancakes cooked on one side only. As they are cooked remove from the pan and place on greased paper with cooked side up.

Spread each pancake with chicken mixture and roll up.

Place on a greased ovenproof dish, sprinkle with cheese and brown under a hot grill.

CHEESE PUDDING

3 servings – (each serving 10g carbohydrate 252 cals)

Ingredients
2 eggs
4 oz grated cheese
1 teaspoonful made mustard
1 oz breadcrumbs
salt and pepper
½ pint milk

METHOD

Preheat oven to 350°F (180°C) or Mark 4.

Beat eggs slightly and add cheese, mustard, breadcrumbs, salt and pepper to taste.

Boil the milk, add to the rest of the ingredients.

Pour into a greased ovenproof dish (rubbed with onion), bake for 20 minutes and serve.

CHEESE SOUFFLE

4 servings (each serving 10g carbohydrate 375 cals)

Ingredients
1½ oz butter or margarine
1½ oz flour
¼ teaspoonful mustard powder
½ pint milk
4 oz Cheddar cheese (grated)
seasoning
3 egg yolks
4 egg whites

Grease a medium-sized soufflé dish and tie foil or greaseproof paper on the outside to at least 2 in. above the rim.

Make a roux with the butter, flour and mustard powder, add milk gradually, bring to the boil, season and stir over a low heat until the sauce thickens. Stir in cheese and leave to cool. Separate eggs, and beat yolks, then add to sauce. Beat whites until stiff and fold into mixture. Bake for 40 minutes at 375°F (190°C) or Mark 5.

Remove foil or paper and serve immediately.

CREAM PUFFS

8 puffs – (each puff 10g carbohydrate 190 cals)

Ingredients

2 oz margarine
scant ½ pint water
pinch salt
4 oz plain flour
2 eggs
4 oz double cream

METHOD

Put the margarine, water and salt into a saucepan and bring to the boil.

Reduce heat, add flour and mix well. Cook on a low heat for a few minutes until mixture starts to leave the side of the pan. Remove from heat and allow to cool.

Beat in eggs one at a time and continue beating until mixture is smooth and shiny. (This takes about 10 minutes.)

Pipe on to a greased baking tin to make 8 puffs. Bake at 425°F (220°C) or Mark 7 for 20 minutes.

When cold, cut off top of puffs and fill centres with whipped cream.

DATE AND SPICE CAKE

12 slices – (each slice 15g carbohydrate 122 cals)

Ingredients
    4 oz dates
    3 fl oz water
    5 oz self-raising flour
    2 oz sorbitol
    1 level teaspoonful mixed spice
    1 level teaspoonful bicarbonate of soda
    2 oz margarine
    1 fl oz milk

METHOD

Preheat oven to 350°F (180°C) or Mark 4.

Chop the dates and stew in water for 5 minutes.

Sieve together flour, sorbitol, spice and bicarbonate of soda. Rub in margarine.

Add the dates and water in which they have been cooked also the milk. Mix all ingredients well together and beat for 5 minutes.

Put the mixture into a greased 6-in. cake tin. Bake on the middle shelf of the oven for 35 minutes.

DEVILLED COD

4 servings – (each serving negligible carbohydrate 280 cals)

Ingredients
    2 lb cod
    1 oz margarine
    1 level teaspoonful curry powder
    1 oz tomato chutney
    1 level teaspoonful dry mustard
    seasoning

METHOD

Remove skin and bones from the fish and cut in four.

Place under grill and cook one side only.

Remove from heat and turn over.

Cream margarine and beat in curry powder, mustard, chutney and seasoning. Spread mixture on uncooked side of fish and return to grill until the cod is cooked.

FRUIT CAKE

12 slices – (each slice 15g carbohydrate 160 cals)

Ingredients
- **6 oz self-raising flour**
- **1 teaspoonful bicarbonate of soda**
- **2 oz margarine**
- **4 oz sorbitol**
- **4 oz mixed dried fruit**
- **5 fl oz milk (¼ pint)**
- **5–6 drops orange or lemon essence**
- **2 teaspoonsful vinegar**

METHOD
Preheat oven to 325°F (170°C) or Mark 3.

Sieve flour and bicarbonate of soda into a bowl and rub in margarine. Add sorbitol and dried fruit and mix well. Stir in the milk and essence, add the vinegar and beat for at least 5 minutes.

Grease a 6-in. cake tin, fill with the mixture and bake for 1 hour.

GARNISHED MACKEREL

3 servings – (each serving 5g carbohydrate 200 cals)

Ingredients
- **1 small onion**
- **1 clove garlic or garlic salt (optional)**
- **2 oz mushrooms**
- **1 lb filleted mackerel**
- **¼ oz flour**
- **2 tablespoonsful oil**
- **1 teaspoonful dried mixed herbs**
- **salt and pepper**
- **1 tablespoonful vinegar**

METHOD
Preheat the oven to 275°F (140°C) or Mark 1.

Peel and chop the onion and garlic finely and wipe and slice the mushrooms.

Wash and dry the fish fillets and roll them in the flour.

Heat half the oil and fry the mackerel on both sides until brown, then place in an ovenproof dish and keep warm in a low oven.

Clean the pan, heat the remaining oil and fry the onion until soft.

Add the mushrooms, herbs, garlic and seasoning and continue frying gently for a further 5 minutes.

Pour the vinegar into the pan, bring the mixture to the boil and spread over the fish in the serving dish.

GOOSEBERRY FOOL

4 servings – (each serving 5g carbohydrate 218 cals)
Ingredients
1 lb firm gooseberries
1 cup water
1 oz fructose
1 level teaspoonful gelatine
¼ pint thick cream

METHOD
Wash, top and tail gooseberries and stew with ½ cup water and fructose until soft.

Dissolve gelatine in the remaining water over a pan of hot water. Strain into the gooseberries

Allow to cool, then beat to a purée.

Fold in the cream and chill before serving.

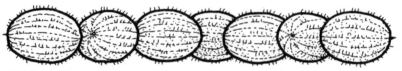

KEDGEREE

4 servings – (each serving 10g carbohydrate 270 cals)
Ingredients
1 lb cooked smoked haddock
2 hard-boiled eggs
2 oz butter or margarine
5 oz cooked long grain rice
seasoning
chopped parsley

METHOD
Flake fish and chop eggs. Melt butter or margarine, add fish, rice, eggs and seasoning. Heat thoroughly over a low heat. Sprinkle with parsley and serve.

MINCED MEAT PIE

2 servings – (each serving 20g carbohydrate 460 cals)

Ingredients

PASTRY
2 oz flour
1 oz lard or margarine
1 tablespoonful water
FILLING
8 oz mince
1 small onion (finely chopped)
2 oz mushrooms
3 fl oz stock or water
1 teaspoonful mixed herbs
1 teaspoonful tomato purée
seasoning

METHOD

Preheat oven to 375°F (190°C) or Mark 5.

Make the pastry with the flour, fat and water.

Fry the mince in a dry pan until lightly browned and transfer to a small pie dish.

Fry the onion in the fat from the mince until soft. Mix with the mince in the dish.

Slice the mushrooms and add to the mixture.

Mix together stock, herbs, tomato purée and seasoning, pour over the mince.

Roll out pastry and cover the top of the dish.

Bake for about 30 minutes.

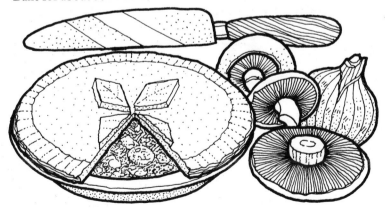

ORANGE CHEESECAKE

6 servings – (each serving 10g carbohydrate 137 cals)

Ingredients

6 small digestive biscuits
1 oz butter or margarine (melted)
8 oz cottage cheese
8 oz low fat natural yogurt
1 small lemon
1 orange plus 6 orange segments
½ oz gelatine
1 oz fructose OR 2 oz sorbitol
1 egg white

METHOD

Crush the biscuits, add to melted butter and mix to a stiff paste. Grease a shallow 7-in. serving dish with butter, and line the dish with the biscuit mixture.

Sieve cottage cheese and blend with yogurt.

Grate lemon and orange rind, extract juice and stir all into cheese mixture.

Dissolve gelatine in 3 tablespoonsful of hot water. Strain into the cheese mixture and stir in the fructose or sorbitol.

Whisk egg white until stiff and fold into mixture. Pour into biscuit base and leave in a cool place to set.

Decorate with orange segments.

N.B. The filling can be made without a biscuit base. The carbohydrate per serving will then be negligible.

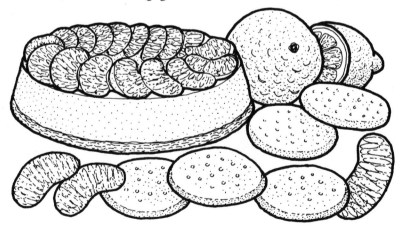

POTATO TART

3 servings – (each serving 20g carbohydrate 280 cals)

Ingredients
10 oz cooked potatoes
1 oz flour
1 oz butter
4 oz lean bacon
2 eggs
5 fl oz milk ($\frac{1}{4}$ pint)
seasoning
1 oz grated cheese

METHOD

Mash potatoes and blend in the flour and butter.

Roll out on a pastry board to about $\frac{3}{4}$-in. thickness. Line an 8-in. flan tin with this pastry and bake at 375°F (190°C) or Mark 5 for about 15 minutes. Remove from oven.

Chop bacon and spread on base of flan. Beat eggs and milk together, season and pour over bacon.

Sprinkle with cheese and return to the oven for a further 25 minutes.

QUICHE LORRAINE

4 servings – (each serving 20g carbohydrate 418 cals)

Ingredients
PASTRY
4 oz flour
1$\frac{1}{4}$ oz lard
1 oz margarine
1 tablespoonful water
pinch salt
FILLING
4 oz cottage cheese
2 eggs
2 fl oz milk
$\frac{1}{2}$ teaspoonful made mustard
1 small onion
2 oz bacon
seasoning
1 tomato
1 oz Cheddar cheese (grated)

METHOD

Preheat oven to 325°F (170°C) or Mark 3.

Make pastry with the flour, lard, margarine, water and salt. Roll out and line a greased 8-in. flan tin.

Sieve cottage cheese and beat it into the eggs, milk and mustard. Peel and slice onion thinly. Trim and cut bacon into strips.

Put bacon into a frying pan with the rinds and fry gently until the fat runs. Add the onion and fry until soft but not brown. Remove the rinds.

Combine the cottage cheese mixture with the onion and bacon, season to taste and pour into prepared flan tin.

Peel and slice tomato and arrange on top. Sprinkle with grated cheese and bake for about 40 minutes, until the flan filling is set and lightly browned.

Serve hot or cold.

QUICK CHICKEN

2 servings – (each serving 5g carbohydrate 232 cals)

Ingredients **½ small chicken**
OR
2 chicken pieces
¼ oz butter or oil
2 oz mushrooms
7 fl oz condensed chicken soup

METHOD

Preheat oven to 375°F (190°C) or Mark 5. Brush chicken with butter or oil and roast in a covered casserole for 15 minutes.

Trim and slice mushrooms and add to the dish. Pour over the undiluted soup and bake with the lid on for a further 20–25 minutes or until the chicken leaves the bones easily.

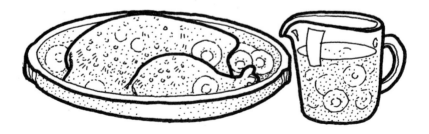

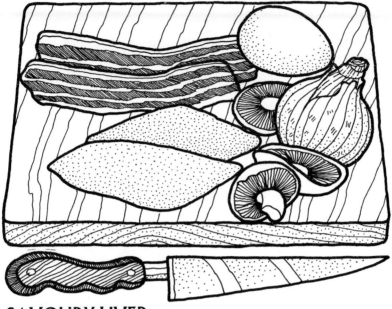

SAVOURY LIVER

4 servings – (each serving 10g carbohydrate 275 cals)

Ingredients
12 oz lambs liver
3 oz bacon
2 oz onion (1 small)
2 oz mushrooms
2 oz soft breadcrumbs
chopped parsley
1 egg
seasoning
5 teaspoonsful Worcester sauce
6 fl oz water

METHOD
Slice liver and put in an ovenproof dish. Remove rind and excess fat from bacon.

Peel and dice onion and mushrooms finely and mix with breadcrumbs and parsley. Bind with beaten egg and season.

Spread mixture over liver and top with bacon slices. Mix sauce and water together and pour over. Cover and bake at 350°F (180°C) or Mark 4 for 1 hour.

SPANISH OMELETTE

2 servings – (each serving 10g carbohydrate 341 cals)

Ingredients

OMELETTE MIX
4 eggs
1½ tablespoonsful water
½ oz butter

FILLING
1 small onion
1 medium tomato
2 oz mushrooms
4 oz boiled potatoes
1 clove garlic (optional)
½ oz butter or margarine
strips of red and green pepper (optional)
seasoning
chopped chives or parsley
1 teaspoonful oil

METHOD

Peel and chop onion and tomato and slice mushrooms. Dice potatoes. Crush garlic.

Heat butter in a frying pan and fry onion, garlic and pepper strips until soft. Add mushrooms, potatoes and tomato and cook for a few minutes. Season to taste.

Set mixture aside to keep hot and wipe pan.

Heat oil and pour in half basic omelette mixture. Lift edges to prevent sticking. When omelette starts to set, spread on vegetable mixture and pour on rest of egg mixture. Put pan under grill and cook until set. Garnish with parsley or chives.

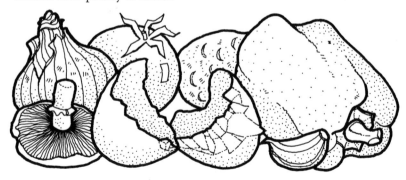

STEW AND DUMPLINGS

2 servings – (each serving 20g carbohydrate 662 cals)

Ingredients

STEW
½ lb stewing steak (trimmed)
1 tablespoonful cooking oil
1 medium onion
2 medium carrots
1 small turnip
stock or water
seasoning

DUMPLINGS
2 oz self-raising flour
½ level teaspoonful baking powder
1 oz suet
little water

METHOD
Cut the steak into chunks and fry in heated oil in a heavy saucepan until lightly browned.

Peel and chop the vegetables and add to pan.

Barely cover with stock or water and season to taste.

Cover pan and simmer very gently for about 1½ hours.

TO MAKE DUMPLINGS Mix flour, baking powder and suet together and mix with enough water to form a sticky dough. Form into a roll, divide into 4 equal dumplings and add to the stew, continue cooking for a further 20 minutes.

STUFFED TOMATOES

2 servings – (each serving 5g carbohydrate 30 cals)

Ingredients
**4 medium tomatoes
1 small onion or shallot
2 oz mushrooms
tablespoonful oil
½ oz soft white breadcrumbs
2 teaspoonsful fresh chopped parsley or
   mixed herbs
OR
1 teaspoonful dried mixed herbs
seasoning**

METHOD

Preheat oven to 350°F (180°C) or Mark 4.

Wash tomatoes, cut off the tops, remove cores and scoop out the seeds without damaging the shells. Peel and finely chop onion, wipe and slice mushrooms. Heat oil and fry onion until soft, add mushrooms and cook a further 2–3 minutes. Add breadcrumbs, herbs and seasoning, mix well and spoon stuffing into tomato shells. Replace tops. Place on a greased baking tin and bake for about 10 minutes.

TUNA FISH SALAD

4 servings – (each serving negligible carbohydrate 202 cals)

Ingredients
**7 oz can tuna fish
3 hard-boiled eggs
2 spring onions
2 fl oz low calorie mayonnaise
seasoning
lettuce leaves
slices of tomato and cucumber**

METHOD

Drain and discard the oil and flake the fish into a mixing bowl.

Shell and chop the eggs, slice the onions finely, mix with the fish and bind with the mayonnaise. Add seasoning to taste. The mixture improves when chilled for a few hours. Arrange on a serving dish and decorate with the lettuce leaves and cucumber and tomato slices.